KNOWING
THE
TRUTH

A Sociological Approach to
New Testament Interpretation

HOWARD CLARK KEE

225.6
K24k

LIBRARY
ATLANTIC CHRISTIAN COLLEGE
WILSON N. C.

FORTRESS PRESS
Minneapolis

Cover design by David Lott

Biblical quotations, unless otherwise noted, are from the Revised Standard Version of the Bible, copyright 1946, 1952, © 1971, 1973 by the Division of Christian Education of the National Council of the Churches of Christ in the U.S.A., and are used by permission.

COPYRIGHT © 1989 BY AUGSBURG FORTRESS

All rights reserved. No part of this publication may be reproduced, stored in a retrieval system, or transmitted in any form or by any means, electronic, mechanical, photocopying, recording, or otherwise, without the prior permission of the publisher.

Library of Congress Cataloging-in-Publication Data

Kee, Howard Clark.
  Knowing the truth : a social approach to New Testament
interpretation / Howard Clark Kee.
    p. cm.
  Bibliography: p.
  ISBN 0–8006–2335–5
  1. Bible. N.T.—Criticism, interpretation, etc. 2. Bible. N.T.—
Theology. 3. Sociology, Biblical. I. Title.
BS2361.2.K44 1989
225.6—dc19   89–7649
                                                              CIP

Printed in the United States of America   1-2335

For Peter and Brigitte Berger:
Stimulating colleagues and faithful friends
during my years at Boston University

ref. 8.61

JAN 4 7 1990

89-02048

Contents

Preface

The chapters of this book represent issues that have been thought through and formulated in a variety of contexts. Basic have been conversations with students and colleagues in recent years here at Boston University. Other opportunities for consideration of these interpretive questions have come through participation in groups at the national meetings of the Society of Biblical Literature and in discussion sessions with colleagues in the Boston area (including the preparation of and response to my presidential address to the New England Regional American Academy of Religion), and in the New Haven Theological Discussion Group. A presentation on biblical theology at the Pittsburgh Theological Seminary led to the preparation of an essay which appeared in a different form in *Horizons in Biblical Theology* 7/2, and is reproduced here (as chapter 4) by permission of the editor, Dr. Ulrich Mauser. One of the most stimulating opportunities came in the form of the National Endowment for the Humanities Seminar for College Teachers, which I led at Boston University in the summer of 1986. Prof. John E. Stanley, of Warner Pacific College and a member of the Seminar, recorded the initial version of the questions which arose out of the seminar sessions, which I have expanded and incorporated in revised form in chapter 3.

This work is offered as a methodological prologue to a New Testament Theology on which I am currently at work, which seeks to take more fully into account the changing social contexts of nascent Christianity. The book is dedicated, with gratitude for friendship and intellectual challenge, to my esteemed colleagues at Boston University, Brigitte and Peter Berger.

HOWARD CLARK KEE
William Goodwin Aurelio Professor of Biblical Studies
Boston University
December 1988

Introduction

At least since the early eighteenth century, Christian faith has been widely perceived as the way in which individuals enter a right relationship with God. This notion is expressed in a variety of hymns and songs and in a range of cultural contexts, as is evident in a gospel hymn ("I come to the garden alone. . . . And he walks with me and he talks with me, and he tells me I am his own") or in a spiritual ("Just a little talk with Jesus makes it right," or "Jesus, hold my hand") or in a song of inspiration ("My God and I, we walk the fields together"). In spite of differences in cultural sophistication, all these popular expressions of faith are united in considering the essence of faith to consist of an individualistic, that is, one-to-one relationship with God through Jesus. It is the thesis of this book, however, that this perception of Christianity in its origins is directly contradicted by the study of the New Testament— the New Covenant—which sets out the ways that Jesus and the movement to which his words and works gave rise sought to redefine participation in the community of God's people.

This individualistic tendency has been an important feature of American culture broadly, from the days when those in search of personal and religious freedom fled to the shores of America. It has been reinforced by the "rugged individualism" of much of American politics, and was a major factor in the pioneering movements of the nineteenth century. In the later twentieth century it has found expression in periodic outbursts of antiestablishment activities, and is evident in the statistics that show the simultaneous massive decline in membership in the more traditional churches and the growth in those religious groups which emphasize freedom of personal display, such as charismatic movements, nondenominational churches, and TV churches.

Continuation of the individualistic religious preference has been reinforced in the scholarly study of religion by the welcome accorded in America to the German intellectual school of thought often designated as the history-of-religions school. Some of the

1

intellectual developments of the nineteenth century which shaped this school of thought will be traced below (chap. 2), but here it will suffice to note some of its effects on the method of interpretation of the New Testament which has been dominant in Germany and America until the 1970s.

In Europe of the late eighteenth and early nineteenth centuries there were constructive responses to the rationalistic mood of the so-called Enlightenment (late seventeenth–early eighteenth centuries), which sought to replace the concepts of the supernatural and of revealed religion with rational, humanly developed theories of the origins of the universe and of moral responsibility. Two major figures who subsequently offered alternatives that allowed for the existence of God and the operation of spiritual powers within the universe were Immanuel Kant (1724–1804) and G. W. F. Hegel (1770–1851). Kant taught that the moral imperative that God had established in the universe was perceived only imperfectly in human precepts and institutions, but that it was indeed binding on human beings. One of the results of Kant's theory was to lead religious thinkers to search for enduring principles that could be discerned behind the various historical systems and concepts that could be found in historical religions, including historic Judaism and Christianity. Hegel elaborated another system, according to which human thought and institutions developed through a system of balanced, opposing forces, which he called "theses and antitheses." The tensions between these factors led to a synthesis, which thereupon elicited a new antithesis. Broad examples of this pairing of reality include spirit versus nature; universal versus particular; ideal versus real.

These two intellectual modes had a direct and enduring effect on the study of religion, including the interpretation of the New Testament and other early Christian literature. As the history-of-religions school of thought developed in the nineteenth century it adopted features of these philosophical theories: (1) It sought to classify the evidence about such religious movements and Judaism in the Hellenistic and Roman periods into categories, many of which were perceived as antithetical to each other; (2) it tried to discern behind the varied phenomena some spiritual insights or principles which transcended the variety of conceptual and institutional forms of religion in Judaism and early Christianity. On the first point, for example, Jewish influences on Christian origins were opposed to the impact of Hellenistic culture. Preaching material (kerygmatic) was set over against instructional material (didactic). Apocalyptic Judaism was contrasted with rabbinic Judaism. Not only are the

2

assumed contrasts inappropriate to the historical evidence, but the concepts, literary modes, and institutional developments of both Judaism and Christianity in this formative period were undergoing constant change, with cultural influences flowing simultaneously in several directions. The history-of-religions approach resulted in an artificial and oversimplified reading of the evidence.

An equally serious flaw was the assumption of this intellectual tradition that behind the enormously variegated phenomena of these religions at the turn of the eras were certain timeless ideas and principles. The historian was obligated to discern and extract these principles and eternal ideas from the culture-bound concepts and literary forms in which they were expressed. Down into the present century these intellectual theories have exerted a powerful influence, not only in Germany where they arose, but in America as well. For example, at the turn of this century the great church historian, Adolf von Harnack, in a popular book, *Das Wesen des Christentums* [*The Essence of Christianity*][1] reduced Christianity—whose rise and spread he had described in huge, complex volumes—to three principles: the fatherhood of God, the brotherhood of man, and the infinite worth of the human soul.

In the 1920s and 1930s similar reductionist views of Jesus and early Christianity were advanced by scholars in America and in Germany. As early as 1914 at the University of Chicago, Shirley Jackson Case, in *The Evolution of Early Christianity*,[2] depicted religion in general as the outcome of spiritual attainments by the individual. These are said to be conditioned by one's surroundings, colored by one's personality, and measured by the vigor of one's religious activity. Christianity was not to be viewed as a divine insertion into history, but as an outburst of spiritual energy on the part of Jesus and his followers as they strove for new and richer religious attainments in response to stimuli that derived from a newer and more suggestive environment.[3] Case's colleague Shailer Matthews similarly claimed to be using sociohistorical methods in the analysis of the origins of Christianity, but in fact his aim was to differentiate the historically relative words of Jesus from the eternal principles implicit in them. Matthews's primary interest was in what he called the "social psychology" of Jesus, which he depicted as a revolution that was to be achieved through a divine family motivated by love, rather than by violence.[4] His work shows little interest in the sociocultural setting in which Jesus lived and taught, and the conclusions he reached are very similar to the broad, pious generalizations of von Harnack, which are noted above.

Meanwhile, in Germany the essence of the message of Jesus received analogous formulation in a work by Rudolf Bultmann, *Jesus,* which was translated into English under the title *Jesus and the Word.*[5] In this reconstruction of the central message of Jesus, Bultmann described the essence of Jesus' message to his followers as the call to decision—for or against the will of God. By advancing this hypothesis Bultmann was conforming the message of Jesus to the philosophical viewpoint of Martin Heidegger, whose existentialism portrayed human existence as making decisions in the face of death, humanity's inscrutable, inescapable destiny. Such a decision could lead to fulfillment or disaster; what was essential was the courage to decide. Bultmann adapted this as a way of understanding the message of Jesus: he called his followers to obey God, even though the consequences might be rejection or death, confident that God would ultimately vindicate this decision of faith. Jesus was the prototype of this decision making, in his obedience unto death. The resurrection was viewed by Bultmann as a way of understanding and accepting such radical obedience, and of seeing in the larger perspective the enduring benefit of such a decision.

It is ironic that Bultmann should have depicted the essence of Jesus in such a radically individualistic way, since in his other scholarly writings Bultmann emphasized the life situation of the sayings of Jesus and the stories about them. In his analysis of the Gospels and their supposed oral sources he was a pioneer in the form-critical method, which sought to discern the formal patterns in which the sayings and narratives incorporated in the Gospels had been preserved before they were incorporated in the written form in which we find them in the Gospels. These forms included various types of brief stories about Jesus, as well as the forms of the teachings attributed to him, which ranged from isolated sayings to parables.[6] Bultmann, however, was concerned more with the setting in which the Gospel sayings and narratives had been recorded and transmitted than with the possible situations in which they may have originated in the life of Jesus. Indeed, apart from Jesus' baptism and death, Bultmann had little confidence in the Gospel accounts of the career of Jesus. Although his announced goal was the reconstruction of what he called the *Sitz im Leben* (life situation) of the Jesus tradition in the context of the Palestinian or Hellenistic church, his real interest was the radically individualistic call to decision which was the essence of Jesus' message to his contemporaries.

The powerful appeal of this understanding of the message of Jesus as fundamentally individualistic is perhaps best exemplified in a comparative study of Judaism and Christianity written in the 1950s by the venerable Jewish philosopher-theologian Martin Buber, who was lecturing in this country just prior to the publication of his book, *Two Types of Faith*.[7] In his lectures, one of which I was privileged to hear, he set out one of his basic theses: that Judaism was the religion of the community, while Christianity was the religion of the individual. I found this distinction to be historically and theologically unsatisfactory, and in the question period following the lecture I asked Professor Buber to identify his source for this depiction of Christianity as individualistic. He replied, "The writings of Rudolf Bultmann." I was not surprised by his naming Bultmann as the source for this historical judgment, but I was relieved to find that Buber did not attempt to document his position by appeal to the New Testament or other early Christian writings.

In American Protestantism that is far removed from the lofty intellectual levels of Bultmann or Buber the individualistic perception of Christian faith is pervasively evident. It is perhaps not surprising that the Bultmannian version of the gospel as a one-to-one relationship with God was quickly and widely adopted by Protestants in America, especially among those whose tradition emphasized personal religious experience.

Discoveries of Jewish documents from the first century C.E., such as the Dead Sea Scrolls, however, as well as fresh assessment of such ancient Jewish materials as the Mishnah and Talmud—especially in the extensive writings of Jacob Neusner on what he felicitously calls "formative Judaism"—have led to a radical rethinking of postbiblical Judaism. It is now evident that the major issue in Judaism from the time of the return of the Israelites from captivity in Babylon—especially in the two centuries before and after the birth of Jesus—was: What are the criteria for participation in the covenant people? This question was fiercely debated between the Jewish nationalists, the priests, and those Jews who had in some degree assimilated to Hellenistic culture, on the one hand, and dissident groups such as the Dead Sea community and the Pharisees, on the other. Although an act of decision could align the individual with one or another of these competing factions within Judaism in this period, the outcome of the decision was a mode of community identity.

We shall see how the early Christians addressed these options. But it is imperative that we, as those engaged in historical inquiry, take as full an account as possible of the varied social contexts out of which our evidence comes, instead of imposing on the historical evidence the categories and values of our own intellectual setting, with the grand assumption that in some way our methods are timeless and provide us access to eternal, unchanging truth. Both what we are investigating and the intellectual methods by which we investigate are social in nature. What we are examining are modes of social identity, by which people saw themselves as sharing in the covenant people. And the strategy of this examination must take into account that human knowledge itself is the socially shared phenomenon in both its experiential and its cognitive dimensions. We shall see that those who were persuaded that God's truth was uniquely revealed to his people through Jesus grasped that truth in terms of the social and cultural context out of which their response came. Hence the title of this book, *Knowing the Truth*.

The task of this volume will be to examine the social nature of human knowledge, since the fundamental question of how knowledge occurs is an issue not only for students of religion but also for the whole range of intellectual inquiry. In chapter 1, analysis is concentrated on what are often called the human and social sciences, and the excursus to this chapter traces related developments concerning knowledge theory in the natural sciences. The aim is to show that knowledge—throughout the range of human inquiry—is social in nature and oriented within a community sharing convictions and assumptions. This is the case in the natural sciences among those who are aware and critical of the nature of human knowledge, and it therefore ought to be self-consciously the case in the study of religion. It is an approach which should be regarded as essential among those who take seriously the claim of the writer of the Pastorals, who asserts that God desires all human beings "to come to the knowledge of the truth" (1 Tim. 2:3-4). It is surely a prerequisite for those who engage in the interpretation of the New Testament.

Chapter 2 offers a survey of recent developments in New Testament interpretation, with special attention given to ways in which social-science studies have contributed to the analysis of the social context of early Christianity. Chapter 3 provides a brief sketch of how the social sciences can be used to extract new interpretive information from the early Christian texts through interrogation. Chapter 4 illustrates the ways in which this approach to New Testament interpretation illuminates the range of social, cultural, and theological responses to Jesus. Also illuminated are the variety of communal forms assumed by those who, in different social and cultural contexts, saw themselves to be the New Covenant people and who were persuaded that Jesus was God's agent for covenant renewal. What is suggested here is a new approach to New Testament theology.[8]

=1=

A Social Science Approach to Knowledge for the Study of Religion

Although the term "religious science" is rarely used in American English, there is a tacit assumption that the academic study of religion should match in intellectual rigor research in the natural sciences and social sciences. German modes of speech make the analogies explicit; in parallel with *Naturwissenschaft* (natural science) and *Sozialwissenschaft* (social sciences) there are *Geisteswissenschaft* (the human sciences) and, more specifically, *Religionswissenschaft* (religious science). Implicit in this cluster of assumptions about intellectual rigor is the notion that the natural sciences are dealing with hard data, and that those of us engaged in the religious sciences should seek to emulate our more rigorous colleagues.

Help from the Natural Sciences

Thomas S. Kuhn. Profoundly relevant to these issues is the observation of Thomas S. Kuhn, in *The Structure of Scientific Revolutions*, that the dominant epistemology of the West assumes that sensory experience is fixed and neutral, so that theories are simply humanly formulated interpretations of given data. Although he is unable to relinquish this view entirely, he finds it seriously inadequate.

Science, Kuhn insists, always juxtaposes a particular set of experiences with a particular paradigm, so that no pure observation language has ever been devised. As he puts it, "No language . . . restricted to reporting a world fully-known in advance can produce mere neutral and objective reports of 'the given.' " The choice of the interpretive paradigm itself determines large areas of experience. Kuhn then illustrates his points by showing that, after the

7

development of atomic theory, "chemists came to live in a world where reactions behaved quite differently from the way they had before." Thus, since even the percentage compositions of well-known compounds were different, "the data themselves had changed" and the scientists, subsequent to the change of paradigm, were working "in a different world."[1] In another example, after Kuhn shows how Isaac Newton's new laws of motion and dynamics transformed Galileo's line of inquiry about the heavenly bodies in the cosmos, he notes that it is changes of this sort "in the formulation of questions and answers" which, far more than empirical discoveries, "account . . . for major scientific transitions."[2]

Initially the paradigms in the natural sciences are simply presupposed: research seeks clarification and precision of measurement, as well as elimination of problematical aspects. These determine what is regarded as normative science.[3] Then certain inadequacies of "fact" and theory appear, with the result that the paradigm comes to be seen as an anomaly, requiring therefore a change of paradigm, change of observational and conceptual recognition, and change of research categories and procedures. Such radical shifts are accompanied by resistance and professional insecurity.[4] It is not the case that "theories emerge to fit facts that were there all along. Rather, they emerge together with the facts they fit from a revolutionary reformulation of the preceding scientific tradition." The result is that paradigm testing takes place as a "competition between two rival paradigms for the allegiance of the scientific community." Yet proponents of competing paradigms fail to engage each other because of disagreement about the problems that the paradigm is to resolve. Although new solutions often use the vocabulary and apparatus of the old, they do not employ them in the traditional way, so that new relationships among the factors have to be developed. Kuhn illustrates this point in his contrast of the space concepts of Euclid and Einstein, and concludes that "the whole conceptual web has to be shifted and relaid; a whole new way of regarding the problems and the factors in their solution emerges." The tensions are increased because proponents of competing paradigms are operating in different worlds, so that "the transfer of allegiance from paradigm to paradigm is a conversion experience that cannot be forced."[5]

In the 1969 postscript to his epochal work, Kuhn remarks that he has been using "paradigm" in two senses: (1) the detailed model on which the research is based, and (2) the worldview that is implicit in the model. He suggests, therefore, that those who hold incommensurable viewpoints be thought of as members of different language communities, and that their communications problems be analyzed as problems of translations. "In the metaphorical sense no less than in the literal sense of seeing, interpretation begins where perception ends. . . . What perception leaves for interpretation to complete depends drastically on the nature and amount of prior training and experience." As a result, debates over competing paradigms turn, not on logical process, but on premises.[6] If translation is undertaken, it may allow "participants in a communications breakdown to experience vicariously something of the merits and defects of each other's points of view," which can result in "persuasion and conversion." Although he thinks that later theories are better able to solve puzzles than older ones, he rejects the ontological claim that theory is progressing toward some ultimate, objective reality. The postscript ends with an appeal to "corresponding communities in other fields," which takes the form of a series of questions which we might do well to raise in our field of religious science: "How does one elect or is one elected to membership in a particular community, scientific or not? What does the group see collectively as its goals; what deviations, individual or collective, will it tolerate?" Kuhn's concluding observation is that "scientific knowledge, like language, is intrinsically the common property of a group or nothing at all. To understand it we shall need to know the special characteristics of the groups that create and use it."[7]

Ludwik Fleck. In 1979 there appeared in translation from the German a treatise written more than forty years earlier by Ludwik Fleck, a Polish historian of medicine, under the title *Genesis and Development of a Scientific Fact*.[8] In his foreword to Fleck's work Kuhn notes that in traditional science's view of itself, "a fact is supposed to be distinguished from transient theories as something definite, permanent, and independent of any subjective interpretation by the scientist." This kind of epistemology only regards as reliable "the well-established facts of everyday life, or those of classical physics." Kuhn declares that "valuation based on such an investigation is inherently naive."[9] The extended example of changing medical theory which Fleck offers concerns the nature and treatment of syphilis. He shows that what were regarded as the facts that emerged from laboratory investigation of the disease varied with the social theory of the investigators. Fleck concludes that "all

9

empirical discovery can therefore be construed as a supplement, development or transformation of thought style." From this arise facts: "At first there is a signal of resistance in the chaotic initial thinking, then a definite thought constraint, and finally a form to be directly perceived. A fact always occurs in the context of the history of thought and is always the result of a definite thought style." It is shared by a "thought collective," which is characterized by common "problems of interest, judgments that seem evident, and methods used as means of cognition." Since it belongs to a community, the thought style undergoes social reinforcement, with the result that a stylized solution to a problem is perceived as "truth." This is not mere convention, but in historical perspective is an event in the history of thought, and in its contemporary context is a stylized thought constraint. That is, there is within the community a "signal of resistance" which opposes free, arbitrary thinking, and which is called a "fact." Every fact must be in line with the interests of its thought collective, just as the patterns of "resistance"—that is facts—must be effective there as well, and must be expressed in the style of the thought collective. In enduring communities, the communication of thoughts, irrespective of content or logical justification, leads for sociological reasons to the corroboration of the thought-structure. The words used in this process take on special connotations indigenous to the community.[10] For Fleck, any kind of cognition is a social process. Facts arise and are known only by virtue of the given thought style characteristic of a given thought collective.[11] (For further observations on the significance of this approach to knowledge in the natural sciences, see the excursus at the end of this chapter.)

Scientific Epistemology and the Sociology of Knowledge

It is apparent from this overview of two converging approaches to inquiry in the natural sciences that not only is the interpretation of "facts" conditioned fundamentally by the community in which the investigation is being carried out, but even what are to be identified as facts are determined by the scientific paradigm accepted and operative within the community. The basic compatibility of this approach to scientific knowledge with the wider field of sociology-of-knowledge is immediately apparent, even though the sociologists-of-knowledge are more concerned with common sense than scientific inquiry. This development in sociology, which began as a kind of byproduct of the philosophical work of Max Scheler, was given its classic formulation by Karl Mannheim, and then refined by Alfred Schutz.[12] Schutz's impact on Luckmann and Peter Berger is evident in their joint and independent writings, particularly in Berger and Luckmann, *The Social Construction of Reality*,[13] and in Berger's *The Sacred Canopy*.[14]

It may be useful to summarize briefly the world-building process which Berger describes. The first step is *externalization*, which is the process by which a human being establishes an ongoing relationship with the natural world and with the surrounding culture. He or she does not simply accept the world, but forms it, by reproducing "the firm structures for life that are lacking biologically," which is what then constitutes culture. This includes language and society, and, through language, humanly produced symbols, so that all components of culture are shaped socially, be they language, tools, values, or human activities.

The second step is *objectification*. Once structured, society and culture become something "out there"; that is, they stand in human consciousness outside the subjectivity of the individual. As Berger phrases it, "The humanly produced world attains the character of objective reality." Having invented language, humans are dominated by its conventions, syntax and grammar. Having determined values, guilt arises or punishment follows if these are contravened. The cultural world, which was collectively produced, remains real by virtue of collective recognition, with the result that society is able to direct, sanction, control, or punish the conduct of the individual.

Once these objective structures come to determine the subjective structures of consciousness, the third step, *internalization*, takes place. Since socialization is the method by which society transmits its meaning and teaching from one generation to the next, each individual within each new generation must learn to live in accordance with these structures, to identify with them, to allow them to shape her or his life and her or his sense of personal identity.[15]

Consciousness of this world is built up in the individual through conversation with what Berger calls "significant others," especially parents and teachers. In this process, the world functions as both subjective and objective reality—until it is challenged or threatened. In a stable situation, language is the medium by which the individual discerns the *nomos* (law or custom), in terms of which the cognitive and normative edifice is built and maintained. The individual will to some degree shape that world, and to some extent will retain private opinions which diverge from the social norms. But to the extent that the norms are appropriated, *nomos* is the ground of individual identity. Accordingly, "society is the guardian of order and meaning not only objectively in institutional structures, but subjectively as well, in its structuring of individual consciousness."[16] Conversely, radical separation from or challenge to that *nomos* leads to *anomy* or chaos, which may take the form of insanity, meaninglessness, or terror. But when the established norms are taken for granted, the meanings of the individual, of society, and of the universe merge, with the result that *nomos* and *cosmos* are coextensive. When the stability of cosmos is affirmed, it finds expression in a sacred mode, whereby the order is seen to be the function of an awesome power, which, though other than human, is related to human existence. The sacred may be seen in the extraordinary, but can be discerned in ordinary events as well, and is affirmed in the form of rituals. Conversely, chaos is a threat to that divine order: "The sacred cosmos, which transcends and includes [human beings] in the ordering of reality, thus provides [them with] the ultimate shield against the terror of *anomy*."[17]

In *The Social Construction of Reality*, Berger and Luckmann discuss what happens in a society when deviant forms of the universe are proposed, so that not only do heretical views pose a threat to the symbolic universe, but the institutional order is in danger of being violated. This will likely result in repressive measures by the custodians of the official order, as well as in modification of the official formulations in order to combat what is seen as error. When alien societies confront each other, the result is that both sides seek to define their universe over against the other. The conceptual machineries employed to maintain the universe include mythology, theology, philosophy, and science. The first of these depicts the continuities between divine and human activities; the second tries to mediate between the divine and human conceptually; the third focuses on eternal structures as humanly perceived; the fourth concentrates on description of the perceived world. In order to deal with deviants, the guardians of *nomos* engage in: (1) some form of therapy, such as exorcism or instruction to avoid emigration; (2) nihilation, which denies or transforms the claims of the opposing universe; (3) universe maintenance by social organization, through the installation of knowledge experts and of institutional and credal patterns to achieve conformity. When the challenge from the competing symbolic universe is successful, conversion results.[18]

Further Implications for the Social Sciences

Barry Barnes, a sociologist at Edinburgh University, has shown in detail the implications for the social sciences of Kuhn's insights into the social context of paradigms in the natural sciences in his study, *T. S. Kuhn and Social Science*.[19] Barnes characterized Kuhn's view of scientific work as carried out not "by a number of isolated individuals interrogating nature without preconception or biases" but as a "collective enterprise of puzzle-solving, with the evolution of findings depending upon conventionally based communal judgment. . . . Training is socialization; it transmits not the unique patterns inherent in physical nature, but the patterns of conventions constitutive of a sub-culture" (19). He is persuaded that Kuhn's approach not only exemplified good historical method, but is also exactly what is needed for sociological study: "An anthropologist addresses the members of an alien culture just as Kuhn treats historical agents. He assumes that the alien discourse is coherent and meaningful; he seeks to understand it in its own terms, avoiding ethnocentric evaluations and misleading analogies with his own culture; he reads social and cultural change forward from past to present. . . . Sociology is a subject with a naturalistic, rather than a prescriptive or normative orientation; it simply tries to understand the convictions and the concepts of different cultures as empirical phenomena" (5).

As we have seen with Kuhn's own work, Barnes's observations have important implications for the self-understanding and the methods of the historian as well as for the analysis of the social context from which the historical evidence derives. In contrast to the claims of historical positivists or self-styled realists, he declares that "at no point is cognition intelligible as a manifestation of 'reason' or 'logic' alone; at no point does an addition to knowledge correspond purely and simply to a further aspect of reality itself. What it is possible to think and to know is to an extent prestructured. Whatever attains general credulity does so through processes involving cognitive commitments, acquired through socialization and maintained by the application of authority and forms of social control" (11). These patterns of assumptions are fostered and confirmed through the shared language: "There is a sense in which all the specific goals and interests associated with a form of culture are furthered by a usage which gives priority to what comes automatically and unthinkingly to its members. This usage stocks the similarity relations with shared particulars, making good the losses of particulars from the communal memory, and ensuring that the similarity relations stay shared, and that there is no degeneration towards the impossibilities of private language." He goes on to characterize this inclination to preserve the values and goals of the culture by means of the language which is shared and passed on as tending toward "conditions of maximum cognitive laziness," and as manifesting itself in the "incessant twittering of conversation" which is undirected and meandering, but which maintains the communal character of similarity relations.[20] In current culture in the United States, this is apparent in such clichés as "Y'know" and "You know what I am saying," which are repeated with maddening frequency.

In the academic community, Barnes notes, at a more sophisticated level there is a comparable commitment to the shared patterns of axioms and procedures: "Once a particular pattern [of scientific understanding] has emerged, vested interests are immediately generated which tend to maintain it. . . . Accepted laws and definitions become emblems of prestige and standing as well as technical resources." Interest in prediction and control is as strong among scientists as among ideologists; the latter have no monopoly on social or political goals.[21]

Two leading contemporary anthropologists exemplify well the approach to sociological analysis that Barnes is calling for: Clifford Geertz and Mary Douglas. And in both cases, their work has direct bearing on the study of religion, especially in its historical dimensions. Geertz, building on and modifying an insight of Talcott Parsons, understands thought to consist in the construction and manipulation of symbol systems, which are employed as models of other systems: physical, organic, social, and psychological. The aim is to discover how they may be expected to behave or, as we would say, "to be understood."[22] A symbol system is created by human beings—shared, conventional, learned, ordered—and provides them with a meaningful framework for orienting themselves to one another, to the world around them, and to themselves.[23] Since this symbol system is central to the social and self-understanding of the individual, it is also essential for the scientist who is trying to understand an alien culture. Geertz's advice to those thus engaged is as follows: "It is not by storming the citadel of savage life directly, seeking to penetrate their mental life phenomenologically (a sheer impossibility) that a valid anthropology can be written. It is by intellectually reconstituting the shape of that life out of its covered 'archaeological' remains, reconstructing the conceptual system that, from deep beneath its surface, animated it and gave it form."[24] In this connection, Geertz notes that the profound and enduring disillusionment experiences by Claude Lévi-Strauss when he visited a previously unknown tribe was the result of a basic lack: he did not understand their language. Given the fundamental function of language as not only a social medium but as the instrument of identity and group continuity, the linguistic lack in Lévi-Strauss's approach was fatal. He turned instead to a metaphysical position, based on the notion of paired opposites (up/down, left/right, war/peace) which are supposed to provide a "depth interpretation" of human existence, but which in Geertz's view are "far-fetched enough to make even a psychoanalyst blush."[25] Geertz's own recognition of the central role of symbol systems provides a potentially fruitful orientation for the interpreter, as well as an approach for analysis of an alien culture—including one from the ancient past.

Although she does not explicitly appeal to the sociologists-of-knowledge for use of the term "symbolic universe," Mary Douglas asserts the primacy of symbol systems for personal identity: "Symbols are the only means of communication. They are the only means of expressing value; the main instruments of thought; the only regulators of experience. For any communication to take place, the symbols must be structured." She then continues on a subject which is directly relevant to our concerns: "For communication about religion to take place, the structure of the symbols must be able to express something relevant to the social order."[26] The symbols of which she writes are not merely conceptual or visual, however. The image of society that is most significant is not architectural but organic: the human body, with its complexity of functions and forms. Of central importance are its boundaries, its discharges, and its danger zones.[27] The ritual of purification is a way of ordering the whole of life, indeed, of the universe and the place of human beings within it, and especially of the culture within which one finds personal identity. Through the symbolic medium of the physical body, ritual works to maintain the stability and proper functioning of the body politic.[28] Thus bodily blemishes or discharges are regarded as impurities, and therefore as threats to the welfare of the group in which one finds identity.

In *Natural Symbols* and more recently in *Essays in the Sociology of Perception*, Mary Douglas has proposed a typology by which to perceive how various visions of society are selected and maintained. She sees two dimensions of social structure: group and grid. The former has to do with the level of commitment to a society on the part of the members; the latter, with the degree of control exercised by the group. In oversimplified form, the range of possibilities looks like this:

1. low grid/low group: individualism
2. high grid/low group: a complex society in which roles are assigned and accepted
3. low grid/high group: factionalism, in which only the external boundary is clear; all other statuses are open and subject to negotiation.
4. high grid/high group: an institution where hierarchy is respected and loyalty is rewarded.

In order to make sense of the surroundings, the individual looks for principles of guidance in ways sanctioned by the group, in order to justify self to self, and self to others. The pattern that the group takes is not a natural development, but the product of social interaction.[29] Within an incipient religious movement like Christianity—as well as within postbiblical Judaism—examples may be found that cover the spectrum of Mary Douglas's fourfold typology. In her extended discussion of purity under the Levitical code of ancient Israel,[30] and elsewhere in her writings, she is explicit in affirming the direct links between social identity, religious convictions, and ritual obligations. Expanding on Durkheim's aphorism that "society is God," she asserts that "in every culture where there is an image of society it is endowed with sacredness," or conversely that the idea of God can only be constituted from the idea of society.[31] Underlying and confirming the group's assumptions about reality is the shared language, which provides the basis for shared experience articulated in both its simple, everyday forms and in the elaborate speech code which is used in prayer, ritual, and recital of the common tradition. It is this network of convictions and commitments which serves as the foundation on which the social reality is constituted.[32]

Related Developments in Philosophy and Linguistics

In contrast to Wittgenstein's earlier work (the *Tractatus Logico-Philosophicus*), in which he portrayed language as comprised of signifiers on the analogy of pictures, in his later writings[33] he represents language as a form of life, which operates as a "language game." By this he implies that there is an agreed-upon set of rules (or assumptions) which in any given community and at any given time are simply taken for granted. The examples that he adduces include giving and obeying orders, constructing an object from a description, reporting an event, forming and testing a hypothesis, presenting the results of an experiment, making up and presenting stories, plays, songs, jokes, solving arithmetic problems, asking, thanking, greeting, cursing, praying. He contrasts the multiplicity of the tools of language and the ways in which they are used with the abstract formulas that logicians have uttered about the structure of language—including Wittgenstein himself in his *Tractatus Logico-Philosophicus*. In the collection of insights on aphorisms published under the title, *On Certainty*, he describes knowledge as a language game, based on assumptions and inherited traditions, with its convictions anchored in all one's questions and answers.[34] As epitomized by Anthony Kenny in his study of Wittgenstein, the earlier notion (as in the *Tractatus*) that a sentence is a picture is replaced by the view that the meaning of a sentence is determined by the circumstances in which it was uttered and the language game to which it belongs.[35]

The implications for New Testament interpretation of Wittgenstein's view of language have been spelled out in an illuminating way by Anthony Thiselton.[36] He traces the implications for the interpretive task of Wittgenstein's insights concerning the social basis of language: (1) the opening-up of a perspective which allows the interpreter to notice what has always been there to be seen; (2) the shift from concern with the generalities of formal logic to the particularities of specific language situations, which may result in a change in understanding of concepts; (3) the recognition that language-games (which Thiselton understands to be based on mutually agreed upon rules, expectations, limits, and expressed in a shared language) are grounded in human life and activities, which are always subject to temporal or historical change; (4) there is no point in seeking for a logical a priori behind the specific social context of training and upbringing which characterize specific communities. As Wittgenstein noted with respect to human language universally, the language of religious experience cannot be purely private, but is part of a shared public tradition and gains intelligibility' because it is anchored in a public history shared by a community. Expecting and believing have meaning only in relation to the experience of others.[37]

17

Knowing the Truth

The implications of Wittgenstein's philosophy of language not only for the social sciences but also for historiography have been spelled out persuasively and illuminatingly by David Bloor.[38] His definition of a language game includes observations which have a direct, solemn bearing on the historical task in general and on biblical interpretation in particular: "The established meaning of a word does not determine its future applications. The development of a language game is not determined by its past verbal form. Meaning is created by acts of use. . . . Use determines meaning." In contrast to the notion of words having timeless, transcendent meanings he coins the term "finitism," which he defines as thinking of meaning as extending as far as, but not beyond, the finite range of circumstances in which a word is actually used, although he does allow for new uses and meanings for a word to emerge in the future.[39] What keeps Wittgenstein's view of language from being too flexible is his recognition that language users are trained in a body of conventionalized practice, according to which locally accepted standards of relevance must be used if communication is to take place. The implications of these insights are equally important for the historian's analysis of ancient evidence and for self-criticism of the historical undertaking, since both the historian and the evidence must be recognized as operating with linguistic conventions whose meaning is relative to the social setting rather than to timeless conceptual models.[40]

The decisions that the interpreter makes about classification of the evidence are dependent on his purposes and the overall pattern of activity of the community where he or she is located, rather than on inherent truths or even experimental demonstrability. What Wittgenstein calls for is description rather than evaluation.[41] How then do new interpretations of the evidence arise? Bloor answers, "When we detect a change in a language game we must look for a shift in the goals and purposes of its players which is sufficiently widespread and sufficiently uniform to yield that change." Confronted by competing usages we should look for rival groups and track down the causes of rivalry; if we see language games merging with one another, we must look for and try to explain the continuities and alliances between their players. When concepts are used within "the bounded territory of a specialist discipline" the enterprise must be guided by a set of local conventions. "There is no meaning without language games, and no language games without forms of life."[42] Even in the case of mathematical procedures, which for many of our contemporaries are the essence of objectivity, their compelling force derives, not from their transcendent status, but from their being accepted and used by a group of people. As Bloor phrases it, "The depth and degree of opposition between different methodologies says more about their proponents than about the inherent relation of ideas that are involved."[43] This depiction of scholarly disagreement will seem thoroughly familiar to those who have observed or participated in faculty discussions as well as in scholarly conferences among those engaged in the academic study of religion.

Bloor ends his work with a plea to take with full seriousness Wittgenstein's insight as to the social nature of language. He calls for a stifling of "the pedantic instincts" to find qualifications for this view of language: "If meaning equals use, then it equals the whole use and nothing but the use." This will involve the whole of the culture, "the whole, turbulent, cross-cutting stream of interests" that are encountered in every human society. And he pleads, "If we are going to describe, then let us really look and see."[44] Thus Wittgenstein's philosophical insights lead away from the abstract, the classificatory, the transcendent modes of analysis and call for analyzing in social context both the evidence under scrutiny and the members of the community engaged in scrutinizing, with as full recognition as can be achieved of the social nature of both the language in which the tradition has been transmitted and the language of the analysts.

Similarly, Nelson Goodman[45] scoffs at the notion that scientists work with unstructured content or an unconceptualized given or a substratum without properties, since "perception without conception is totally blind. Predicates, pictures, other labels, schemata survive want of application, but content vanishes without form. We can have words without a world but no world without words or other symbols" (6). In comparison with artists or other people in daily pursuits—and, we might add, including historians of religion—"the scientist is no less drastic in rejecting or purifying most of the entities and events of the world of ordinary things while generating quantities of filling for curves suggested by sparse data, and erecting elaborate structures on the basis of meager observation. Thus does he build a world conforming to his chosen concepts and obeying universal laws" (15).

Goodman's view of truth appears to be purely relativistic when he writes, "Truth, far from being a solemn and severe master, is a docile and obedient servant. The scientist who supposes that he is singlemindedly dedicated to the search for truth deceives himself. . . . He seeks system, simplicity and scope; and when satisfied on these scores, he tailors truth to fit." Yet he rejects relativism as thoroughly as he scorns fideism: "While readiness to recognize alternative worlds may be liberating, and suggestive of new avenues of exploration, a willingness to welcome all worlds builds none. Mere acknowledgment of the many available frames of reference provides us with no map of the motions of heavenly bodies; acceptance of the eligibility of alternative bases produces no scientific theory or philosophical system; awareness of varied ways of seeing paints no pictures. A broad mind is no substitute for hard work." Knowing is not to be thought of as determining the truth in some absolute sense, but as an increase in "acuity of insight or in a range of comprehension" so that we are enabled to find "features or structures that we could not discern before" and thereby to advance human understanding.[46]

The recurrence in our survey of the term, symbol, is itself a sign of the growing rapport between social scientists and an important aspect of contemporary philosophy. This motif is best represented by the work of Suzanne Langer. In *Philosophy in a New Key* Langer notes the fundamental challenge to the triumph of empiricism represented by the current widespread recognition that our sense data are primarily symbols: "The edifice of human knowledge stands before us, not as a vast collection of sense reports, but as a structure of *facts that are symbols* and *laws that are meanings.*" As the non-discredited notion of the finality of sense-data was the cue of empiricism, the power of symbolism is the cue of the new philosophical epoch of epistemology.[47] In every age and culture language developed through the gradual accumulation and elaboration of verbal symbols, with the result that speech is the symbolic transformation of experience. But in addition to speech, there is another kind of symbolic process which is neither practically nor verbally communicative, but which is effective and communal in its impact: ritual.[48] The fact that belief, myth, and ritual in societies other than our own may appear irrational or monstrous led Grace De Laguna to the conclusion that their purpose was to gain and maintain the social solidarity of the group.[49] Langer prefers to say that ritual reinforces solidarity, rather than creating it. Both the verbal modes of symbolization (from myth to critical analysis) and the nonverbal modes (ritual, dreams, visions, art) are manifestations of the symbol-making and symbol-using which are essential human characteristics. In contrast to fairy tales, myth in the profound social orientation sense is evident when not only the social forces (persons, customs, laws, traditions) are taken into account in the story, but also the cosmic forces which provide the larger context for human existence. This kind of transformation of symbols employs not fiction, but "the supreme concepts of life" which the symbols represent, and "by which men orient themselves religiously in the cosmos."[50]

It is not at all surprising that it is this central theme in Langer's work that is picked up by Clifford Geertz in his *Interpretation of Cultures.* He defines a culture as a historically transmitted pattern of meanings embodied in symbols, a system of inherited conceptions expressed in symbolic forms by means of which human beings communicate, perpetuate, and develop their knowledge about and attitudes toward life. After quoting Langer's assertion that "sign, signification, communication are our [intellectual] stock-in-trade,"[51] Geertz stresses that social anthropology, and especially that part of it concerned with religion, must take seriously into account this insight. What symbols do, he declares, is to function in such a way as "to synthesize a people's ethos—the tone, character and quality of life, its moral and aesthetic style and mode—and their world-view—the picture they have of the way things in sheer actuality are, their most comprehensive ideas of order." This perception of order is confirmed by ritual, which embodies the authority of the religious perspective by inducing a set of moods and motivations and by defining an image of a cosmic order by means of a single set of symbols, verbal and performatory. The aim of anthropological study is to analyze the system of meanings embodied in symbols and to relate the system to sociostructural and psychological processes.[52]

Similar conclusions have been reached by those in the field of sociolinguistics whose primary concern is the translation of a literature from one language community to another. These insights have been articulated brilliantly in the work of Eugene A. Nida, whose scholarly contribution includes both general translation theory and technical counsel for translators of the Bible throughout the world. On the subject of communication within the framework of society, he writes: "A communication is not intelligible if it is treated as an event abstracted from the social context of which it is a part. Rather, it must be analyzed in terms of its total context, including the relationship of the participants to the [linguistic] code, their relationship to one another as members of the communicating society, and the manner in which the message acts as a link between source [speaker or writer] and receptor [hearer or reader]."[53] The interpreter of the text must, therefore, take fully and critically into account his or her own social setting as well as the relationship to the society in which the communication originated, and above all, the social dimensions of that society.

Implications for the Historical Study of Religion

With the surge of interest in the academic study of religion that began in the 1950s, replacing as it did the predominantly confessional approaches that characterized divinity faculties and church-related colleges, there was a conscious or unconscious turning to what were considered to be the norms of the sciences: objective analysis of concrete evidence, classification of the relevant phenomena, evaluation based on appeal to fixed and logically defensible norms. As we have seen, these ways of knowing are no longer dominant, either in the natural or in the social sciences. Now, in light of the "scientific revolutions" and the basic epistemological shifts that have occurred, the scientific study of religion must abandon the discredited models to which it all too often continues to turn for its methodological base. What is called for? A fundamental change in the modes of knowledge, which include the conscious adoption of new goals, methods, and analytical guides.

Returning to the field of New Testament history and interpretation, which concentrates on historical analysis and the interpretation of ancient texts, we must abandon the effort to force evidence into timeless categories, to weigh it against our own intellectual norms, to seek to discover an eternal essence behind the supposedly useless or outmoded externals of the evidence as it has come down to us. Yet it is precisely that kind of procedure which is being exercised in our field by those claiming to understand the religious past. What is required instead is to seek to enter analytically into the life-world(s) of the communities in and for which the documents and other evidence we possess were produced. This goal cannot be achieved by deciding in advance what life and thought were like in a bygone era. Rather, one must seek sensitivity to attune the mind to interrogate it by means of the questions which were central in the circumstances of the ancient community, rather than those that dominate our own era.

Some examples of the anachronisms and distortions carried on in the name of historical reconstruction may illustrate the seriousness of this methodological problem. Studies purporting to describe the New Testament world treat the important factor of miracle by reference to the figure of Apollonius of Tyana as drawn in the opening years of the third century C.E. by Philostratus. Ignored in this strategy are the facts that the writer was under the patronage of the anti-Christian imperial family, and that much of the story he tells is patently in error (such as places mentioned that were not in fact in existence in the later first century but were allegedly visited by the itinerant philosopher-wonder-worker). But more serious than the failure of some scholars to take into account the time gap between the writing of the Gospels and the time of Philostratus is the failure to notice the important changes in cultural context between these two literatures. Mark's miracle stories, on the one hand, disclose the powerful influence of apocalyptic literature, while the Gospels of Luke and Matthew evidence kinship with Roman historiography and the popular religious romances. Philostratus, on the other hand, is writing in the period of Late Antiquity, so effectively analyzed by Peter Brown as an epoch predisposed to enjoy the occult and the offbeat; he tries to reappropriate a bygone era. It is precisely these features of the cultural climate that Philostratus's reconstruction of the life of Apollonius's travels and performances so dramatically illustrates. They are alien to the first-century Christian world, but are vividly represented in the second- and third-century apocryphal gospels and acts.[54] The interpreter must inquire about the details of the sociocultural context in which these miraculous—or any other—events are reported as having occurred if there is to be understanding of what perspectives are represented in the report.

Akin to this issue is the need to avoid assuming that a word or a concept has a timeless, unchanging meaning, as in the case of *wisdom*, which even in the biblical tradition—canonical and extracanonical—ranges in connotation from proverbial principles (as in the Book of Proverbs) through an equating of wisdom with Torah (as in Sirach) and the accommodation of the law to Hellenistic philosophy (as in Wisdom of Solomon) to wisdom as esoteric disclosure to the faithful (as in Daniel). When the New Testament writers link Jesus with wisdom, one must wonder which of the possible meanings of wisdom is the one in terms of which Jesus is being portrayed.

The literary aspect of historical study has been dominated in recent years by the effort of scholars to interpret texts by means of classifying their genre. Form criticism, as developed by Rudolf Bultmann, is a prime example of this approach, but it has been largely limited to classifications of the sayings of Jesus and the stories about him on the basis of allegedly built-in functions that these genres served in the ancient world. Ignored is the fact that the same media may be employed to a variety of ends; there is no inherent function or value in any genre. Questions must be raised about the intention of the writer, not only in the choice of genre, but in the specific way that the genre is used in a given context. For example, the aphorisms or sayings of Jesus do not automatically identify him as a teacher of timeless wisdom, as is assumed by some scholars working on these issues. The content as well as the intent of the sayings must be analyzed free of unwarranted judgments based on formal observations.

Often unacknowledged, or even unawares, interpreters of ancient texts employ value judgments about the content of the document, with the result that they dismiss as unimportant what was probably essential for the writer of the text and his community. In the reading of the gospel tradition, for example, the modern interpreter may be embarrassed intellectually by the miracle stories and the apocalyptic visions of the gospel tradition in its canonical form. Especially since the discovery of the gnostic gospels, a historical theory has been promulgated that the noncanonical gospels preserve more faithfully the historical Jesus tradition than the canonical gospels do, since in the former there is little if any interest in his activities and his predictions about the future. Instead, Jesus comes across as a teacher of timeless truths for those who are already "in the know." This has an understandable appeal in terms of contemporary intellectual values, but it is scarcely an appropriate ground on which to base what are presented as historical judgments.

Similar to this strategy is the essentialist approach (see the Introduction). It begins by careful analysis of doctrines and claims, some of which are thought to be unacceptable to the modern mind, but it then goes on to differentiate these time-bound oddities from the essential meaning of the documents. Two examples of this approach are the work of the German theologians von Harnack and Bultmann, as we have seen. Each of these scholars made impressive contributions in analysis of the texts under scrutiny in their respective fields, von Harnack for the history of doctrine and Bultmann for the history of the gospel tradition. Yet we have seen that each took an ultimately reductionist stance: von Harnack found the essence of Christianity in a kind of Kantian, Protestant, individualistic piety; and Bultmann found it in Jesus with a similar net result, based on the existentialism of Martin Heidegger. Other forms of reductionism which appeal to different, nonphilosophical bases include the interpreters of the New Testament whose norm for ultimate meaning is provided by the neat pattern of binary opposition set forth by Lévi-Strauss, or those who want to reduce the early Christian writings to demonstrations of patterns developed by formalistic (mis)use of insights from social anthropologists. Sensitivity to differences or to nuances in changing circumstances of the early church is ignored in the drive to reduce the evidence to *alleged* essences.

What is required of historical study, including that of early Christianity, is to be faithful to the evidence as well as the dominant epistemological paradigms in the natural and social sciences. In short, historians and biblical interpreters need to take with full seriousness the distinctiveness of the communities and contexts in which the gospel was heard and responded to in faith. This means, for example, that one must be prepared to distinguish between a community like Mark's, where the insights and values and modes of expression in Jewish apocalyptic have been taken over and adapted to serve the purposes of the writer and his group, and that of the Gospel of John, where the values, modes of expression, and stress on symbolism characteristic of Hellenistic mystical piety predominate. Analogously, the letters of Paul show the significant influence of Stoicism, in ethics as well as in his eschatology, while the Letter to the Hebrews manifests at crucial points Platonic perspectives and terminology. Generalizations about Jewish and Hellenistic influence on the New Testament writers, therefore, must be specified on the basis of concrete texts (cf. chap. 4 below).

Also to be taken into account is the process of social and cultural change which took place in the New Testament period. This is evident in the changing attitudes toward the church—earlier as informal gathering, later as developing institution—as one moves from the authentic letters of Paul to those that stand in the later Pauline tradition. The evidence of both conceptual and structural

ATLANTIC CHRISTIAN COLLEGE
WILSON, N. C.

changes within the life of the early church will be obscured by the widely employed process of classification and categorization.

Instead, what is demanded is awareness of and sensitivity concerning what Jean Piaget has called "the transformation of structures."[55] In the study of the interaction between human beings and their environment one can discern the ways in which traditional patterns of behavior and expression, as well as of social roles and relationships, undergo basic changes. Even when the verbal designations remain the same, the connotations and the networks of human relationships are transformed. To become aware of these processes demands careful assessment of the evidence, with full attention to the earlier forms of the tradition, to the social and cultural forces which contributed to the change, and to the resultant transformations. In such an enterprise there is no place for unchanging concepts, for fixed patterns or literary genres. The primary focus must be on the social context in which the transformation occurred. As Piaget has expressed it in his essay on epistemology, "Human knowledge is essentially active. To know is to assimilate reality into systems of transformations."[56]

It must be acknowledged, of course, that this analytical enterprise, like all other human activities, is itself socially conditioned by the models developed in the wider intellectual community. But perhaps it will suffice to paraphrase the words of Nelson Goodman's suggestion that at least this approach to human understanding may make a modest contribution to clarity.

Excursus: Further Implications of the Paradigm Shift in the Natural Sciences

As we have seen, the shift of the approach to knowledge from the older objectivism of the natural sciences is evident in such diverse fields as sociology, anthropology, linguistics, but also in hermeneutics and history. Yet there is a deep-seated suspicion among academics that what we have referred to as "religious sciences" are intellectually inferior to the natural sciences. It may be useful, therefore, to survey some other explorations of this issue in the natural sciences. Two perceptive studies of models and methods in the natural sciences are those by Richard Bernstein, *Beyond Objectivism and Relativism*[57] and Ian Barbour, *Myths, Models and Paradigms.*[58]

A Social Science Approach

Bernstein discerns a similarity between Thomas Kuhn's approach to knowledge and that of Aristotle, who differentiates *phronēsis* from other modes of knowledge (*epistēmē* and *technē*) as a "form of reasoning which is concerned with choice and which involved deliberation." Integral to this mode of knowledge are the interpretation and specification of universals that are appropriate to a particular situation. The result is that knowledge thus perceived is "involved in theory-choice" which is a "judgmental activity requiring imagination, interpretation, the weighing of alternatives and the application of criteria that are essentially open." Such judgments need to be supported by reasons, which themselves change in the course of scientific development. "Thus it is not a deficiency that rational individuals can and do disagree without either of them being guilty of making a mistake."

Bernstein contrasts "a model of practical rationality that emphasizes the roles of exemplars and judgmental interpretation."[59] After summarizing with approval Richard Rorty's declaration that it is an illusion to think that there is a permanent set of ahistorical standards which the philosopher or epistemologist can discover and which will unambiguously tell us who is rational and who is not,[60] he goes on to reject the "false dichotomy: either permanent standards of rationality (objectivism) or arbitrary acceptance of one set of standards or practices over against its rival (relativism)." He continues, "To acknowledge that in the future there will be modifications of the standards, reasons and practices we now employ does not lead to epistemological skepticism but only to a realization of human fallibility and the finitude of human rationality."[61] Important for our purposes is a brief reference by Bernstein to a statement by Ernan McMullin that the "unit for appraisal in science is a historical one."[62] When he shifts his focus from scientific understanding to hermeneutics (where he is dealing appreciatively, yet critically, with the work of Hans Gadamer), Bernstein comes back to what he calls the "intellectual virtue," *phronēsis*, which he sees as communal rather than individual, in that ethical principles and universals are shared within the interpreting community.[63]

Departing from the order of subjects announced in the title of his book, Ian Barbour begins with models, thereafter shifting to paradigms and finally to myths. He wants to show the relevance and utility of these factors in the study of religion: "Scientific models are products of creative analogical imagination. Data are theory-laden; comprehensive theories are resistant to falsification and there are no rules for paradigm choices."[64] The drive for falsification, which is evident among positivistic philosophers and natural scientists, Barbour calls a delusion: "Religious paradigms, like scientific ones, are not falsified by data, but are replaced by promising alternatives. Commitment to a paradigm allows its potentialities to be systematically explored, but it does not exclude reflective evaluation" (172). He describes a model as experimental, logical, theoretical, as leading to a theory which accounts for observable patterns, and which is subject to critical realism. What is distinctive about models in religious experience is their subject matter: awe and reverence, mystical union, moral obligation, reorientation and reconciliation, key historical events, order and creativity in the world. These models "evoke the communal adoration, obeisance, awe, devotion, ecstasy, courage—[that is,] the emotive and conative dimensions of human experience—that constitute religious faith [in distinction from] philosophical speculation" (65). It is through these models that we see ourselves and all things, that our experience is understood, and that our total environment is illuminated, with the result that there are disclosed to us otherwise unnoticed parallelisms, analogies and patterns among the data which reach us through observation and experience."[65]

Following the lead of Kuhn, Barbour describes paradigms as the defining of a coherent research tradition, or otherwise stated, as articulating the types of questions that may legitimately be asked, the types of explanations that are to be sought, and the types of solutions that are acceptable. Paradigms determine the way one sees the world.[66] Among the reasons for choosing one paradigm over another are predictability, accuracy, simplicity, and fruitfulness.[67] There are no absolute rules for choice among models or paradigms for research programs, but there are independent criteria for assessment of any option.[68]

Barbour rejects both the positivist theory of experience (the private, subjective awareness of sense qualities produced by physical stimuli from the external world) and the corresponding notion about God (as something that is inferred without being experienced). Instead, he insists that the experience of God is expressed in ways analogous to the experience of other selves: through various media of language and action, which are then interpreted by those sharing this experience. Accordingly, members of a religious community understand themselves to be dealing with God.[69] Faith, then, is trust, which is tied to experience and personal involvement, yet is subject to critical reflection, including self-criticism. "Because man searches for coherence, and because his various languages refer to a common world, we cannot rest content with a multiplicity of totally unrelated language games," although any system must be partial and provisional.[70] At the same time, he rejects absolutism, relativism, or the claim that all religions are basically one (whether on deistic, romantic, or other grounds).

The criterion that he proposes for the evaluation of noncognitive functions is the degree to which they fulfill social or psychological needs and provide ethical criteria. For the cognitive functions Barbour prescribes simplicity, coherence, extensibility, and comprehensiveness. He thinks that, while subjective features are more evident in religion than in the natural sciences,[71] the objective features are by no means missing: common data; cumulative evidence; criteria which are not paradigm-dependent. Important for the process, as we have noted, is self-criticism.[72] What he calls for in the academic study of religion is "critical realism," which he contrasts with naive realism, instrumentalism (religion as a useful fiction), and functionalism (religion as a sociological product). He quotes with approval Robert Bellah's championing of "symbolic realism," which expresses feelings and attitudes even while organizing and regulating the flow of interaction between subjects and objects. To this approach through the symbolic world, critical realism adds the analysis of the social context of the religion, as well as its function, shared values, its critical diagnosis of class and social structure, both within and outside the religious community.[73] Thus Barbour comes out where Kuhn and Bernstein do: with the community as the locus of critical inquiry and what is regarded as knowledge resulting from this social process.

Akin to these reassessments of the natural sciences are the insights of Michael Polanyi, who in the post-World War II period made the unusual transition of shifting from the field of physical chemistry (in which he was a professor on the continent and later in Manchester, England) to social studies. His approach was to trace similarities in patterns of knowledge as evident in both the natural sciences and in the wider fields of human inquiry. In his earlier writings he showed the crucial role of the scientific community in recognizing and accepting scientific discoveries, and in evaluating scientific proposals. He depicted scientific research as an art—the art of making certain kinds of discoveries. He stressed the role of the society, which transmits assumptions about the nature of reality through early education and subsequent experience. Verification is achieved and what are regarded as standards of veracity are upheld by a continuous interplay of criticism within the scientific community.[74]

Polanyi rejected the positivist model of science, however, which he described as considering itself a machine that produces universally valid results. He thought science should never claim to be more than an "affirmation of certain things we believe in." These beliefs are to be adopted responsibly, with due consideration of the evidence in support of them, and with a view to universal validity. They are not to be considered as immutable facts or as principles beyond dispute, but as "ultimate commitments, issued under the seal of personal judgment." He emphasized the vital role of the community in transmitting the scientific insights: "We as a community must also face the fact that there is no system of necessary rules which will relieve us of the responsibility of holding the constitutive beliefs of our group, of teaching them to the next generation and defending their continued profession against those who would suppress them."[75] Thus Polanyi asserted the social nature of the affirmations and convictions which are held to be true, and the function of the community in maintaining and transmitting those convictions.

For more than twenty years after the end of World War II, a highly personal book, *The Immense Journey*, written by a leading natural scientist, Loren Eiseley, an anthropologist at the University of Pennsylvania, went through repeated reprintings and attracted a vast readership. The theme of the book was Eiseley's search for the origins of life, in which he explored evidence from geological, paleontological, and marine sources. He wrote:

> Forward and backward have I gone, and for me it has been an immense journey. I have given the record of what one man thought as he pursued research and pressed his hands against the confining walls of scientific method in his time. It is not, I confess . . . , an account of discovery so much as confession of ignorance and of the final illumination that sometimes comes when a man is no longer careful of his pride.[76]

Eiseley went on to acknowledge that the scientific community, in its quest for knowledge of human life and its origins, must rest its case on postulates, not merely on self-validating evidence. "With the failure of these many efforts science was left in the embarrassing position of having to postulate theories of living origins which it could not demonstrate. After having chided the theologian for his reliance on myth and miracle, science found itself in the unenviable position of having to create a mythology of its own: namely, the assumption that what, after long effort, could not be proved to take place today had, in truth, taken place in the primeval past" (199).

The human quest for knowledge, Eiseley makes clear, is not divided into two streams, one of which is objective (the natural sciences) and the other subjective (the human sciences). Both approaches to "the immense journey" are guided by the shared assumptions of the particular community of seekers.

=2

Sociological Approaches to New Testament Interpretation: Survey, Critique, and Proposal

Since the 1960s there has been a proliferation of articles and monographs concerning the use of sociological methods for the study of the New Testament and the historical origins of Christianity. Collectively they display such a diversity in aim and approach as to create a confusing picture. Even some of the earlier bibliographical surveys, valuable as they are, do not offer clear distinctions among the range of strategies for using sociological theory in the historical and hermeneutical analysis of the New Testament.[1] In what follows, I shall attempt to sort out the various types of social analyses of early Christianity:

1. social description;
2. social dynamics and social roles;
3. anthropological analysis and group identity;
4. sociology of knowledge;
5. linguistics and social theory of language (epistemology and hermeneutics);
6. structuralism and deconstructionism.

Here I offer some descriptions of these various theoretical bases and the uses made of them by scholars in religious studies. My aim is to classify these major approaches in order to provide an orientation among the many methodological proposals.

Social Description

On the assumption that understanding of the New Testament and other early Christian writings cannot responsibly be limited to

32

analysis of their theological contents, scholars since early in this century have undertaken to use literary, inscriptional, and archeological resources with the aim of expanding and deepening knowledge of the Greco-Roman world in which Christianity arose. Here the primary interest is in a description of the visible features of the society in which the religion was found: the general economic and social conditions as may be demonstrated or inferred from external evidence. These include social stratification, modes of employment, and the extent of trade and social interchange, for example. Although no one has yet accomplished a study as rich in detail as M. Rostovtzeff's social and economic studies of the Hellenistic and Roman periods,[2] there are useful historical surveys of Judaism in the Greco-Roman world during this period,[3] and of what is broadly designated as "the world of the New Testament."[4] Some of the more ambitious historical studies of Judaism, however, are seriously handicapped by uncritical use of the rabbinic material (second–sixth centuries C.E.) as sources for reconstructing Jewish life and thought in the period before the revolts of 70 and 130 C.E.[5]

Much of the historical study of Christian origins in this century has been carried out with uncritical acceptance of the construct of the late nineteenth-/early twentieth-century German history-of-religions school, as previously noted.[6] This scholarly construct posited that Jesus was a rabbinic figure who sought to call his followers and hearers to direct obedience to God in the land of Palestine where Judaism centered around the twin institutions of temple and synagogue. Hellenistic Judaism, on the other hand, was thought to have been influenced by Hellenistic philosophical speculation and the mystery cults, with the result that it represented a basically different phenomenon. Yet it was in the context of Hellenistic Judaism that the Jesus movement took hold, the theory runs, thereby transforming the picture of Jesus by representing him as wonder-worker and mystic savior rather than as reinterpreter of the law in the rabbinic tradition. It was this hybrid figure of Jesus (so the history-of-religions theory) which caught the attention of the Greco-Roman world. The Jewish type of Christianity that was in direct continuity with Jesus, the mildly reforming prophet, simply died out, yet not before it had created its own portrait of Jesus as an apocalyptic redeemer and had recast the gospel tradition in order to portray him in this role.

Pervasive and persistent as this construction is in New Testament studies, it is an arbitrary framework imposed on the evidence, rather than a program based on sensitive analysis of that evidence and employing critical use of social theory concerning the emergence, growth, and development of religious movements. In contrast with the history-of-religions practice of arbitrary and artificial classification of the material, the sociological method offers the possibility of discovering the fuller sociocultural *Sitz im Leben* of a text or tradition, rather than consigning material to a contrived category.

Following World War II, Robert M. Grant offered an analysis of the social setting of early Christianity. His more recent work has presented details of the demographic, economic, and social dimensions of the Christian movement down through the time of Constantine. Noting the small numbers of converts to Christianity, he infers, "We may not regard [the Christian movement] as a proletarian mass movement but as a relatively small cluster of more or less intense groups, largely middle class in origin."[7] At the time of Constantine's conversion, the aristocracy was predominantly pagan, so that the triumph of Christianity took place from the top down, as Eusebius observed. Grant sketched the range of attitudes of Christians toward the empire, slavery (they did not favor emancipation), and wealth (the flagging of eschatological expectation led to a conservative, aristocratic attitude toward wealth). Important as his historical proposals are, Grant's interests and sources lie in the Constantinian era, rather than in the first-century origins of Christianity. Accordingly, his proposals shed little light on the New Testament materials.

Interest in description of the social setting of early Christianity is central to the work of Abraham J. Malherbe and Wayne A. Meeks. Malherbe's work is in the realm of intellectual history, in that he uses the models of the philosophical schools as a primary basis of comparison for the rise of Pauline Christianity, drawing inferences about the movement on the basis of the linguistic and rhetorical levels of the Pauline writings.[8] He is skeptical about the possibility of drawing inferences from the New Testament writings about the Christian communities by or for whom they were produced.[9] Although he claims to begin with social facts rather than sociological theory, it may rightly be objected that the two cannot be so sharply divided, since the assumption that a "fact" is relevant already carries with it some basic theoretical assumptions which are essential to interpreting the "facts."[10] Sociological theory offers the potential for more precise and profound understanding of the literary and conceptual phenomena, but Malherbe seems to brush aside this potential. His detailed knowledge of philosophical and literary movements within the Greco-Roman world provides important insights and points of comparison for the New Testament scholar, but he gives short shrift to the dimensions of social dynamics, leadership, and social change.

Meeks, on the other hand, is chiefly concerned with the social phenomena of urban life in those centers where Christian groups sprang up in the first century. He draws on the insights of anthropologists Clifford Geertz, Victor Turner, and especially Mary Douglas (see chap. 1 above). His study shows that personal identity based on the social boundaries drawn by Jewish and early Christian groups is a central factor for understanding the issues that shaped the early Christian movement, and that determined its stand on such questions as ritual participation, divorce and marriage, and attitudes toward the state. Questions internal to the group—such as status, authority, decision-making, conflict resolution—may be seen in a clearer light when examined in terms of social theory. In *The First Urban Christians: The Social World of the Apostle Paul,* Meeks seems to dismiss "the village culture of Palestine" which Christianity had left behind "within a decade of the crucifixion of Jesus."[11] But in his most recent work, *The Moral World of the First Christians,* Meeks explicitly develops a sociology-of-knowledge approach, in which he traces the features of the symbolic universe of the "messianic sect" within Israel which became the church. Building on the insights of anthropologists (e.g., Clifford Geertz and Bryan Wilson) and of sociologists (e.g., Peter Berger), he traces the way in which the followers of Jesus and their converts defined themselves over against the then-current options in Judaism for understanding God's purpose for his people. The features of this group included ritual requirements for membership (primarily baptism), stance toward the religious and political leadership of the land, and expectations about God's action to defeat the enemies of his people and establish his rule.[12] This more recent work supplements Meeks's earlier valuable analysis of the social and economic aspects of the movements of Christianity out into the urban centers of the eastern Mediterranean world of the first century.

Significant insights about the dynamics of social existence within the Roman imperial world are offered by Ramsay MacMullen in *Enemies of the Roman Order: Treason, Unrest, and Alienation in the Empire*[13] and *Roman Social Relations 50 B.C. to A.D. 284.*[14] In the first book MacMullen sketches such sociocultural phenomena as itinerant teacher/philosopher/preachers; rulers influenced by popular philosophy; prophets of the end of the present order; the widespread pattern of guilds and voluntary societies; the problems raised by tensions between imperial policy and regional special interests. He notes Rome's generally tolerant attitude toward cultural and religious diversity. In *Roman Social Relations*, MacMullen describes Roman policy concerning rural and village peoples, local assemblies and magistrates, and the tensions arising from rural poverty and the aristocratic exploitation of the farm workers. His description of the class structures of the imperial period shows how power was concentrated in the hands of a few, and therefore how inappropriate it is to employ a modern term such as "middle class" in analysis of Roman society. Social mobility was minimal. Those with shared and fixed social status formed associations to give dignity and purpose to their static mode of existence. Only with the opening of new territories was social and economic change possible. The relevance of all this social description for the rise and spread of Christianity is obvious. Yet in his more recent book, *Christianizing the Roman Empire*,[15] MacMullen concentrates on the fact that by the time of Constantine, conversion to Christianity was socially advantageous, while he fails to explain why persecution and martyrdom were such important factors in the process, or why such a cross section of Roman society—including slaves, members of the mercantile class, and those of the central power group—was attracted to this religion in the first place.

Two other studies of the social nature of early Christianity make important contributions to historical knowledge, and yet both have serious limitations. E. A. Judge's *The Social Pattern of Christian Groups in the First Century*[16] rightly insists on beginning analysis of the New Testament writings by seeking to understand the social situation of the original readers. This involves him in differentiating between the Palestinian groups, grounded in Judaism, among whom Jesus worked and taught, and the Hellenized Jewish and gentile members of the wider urban Mediterranean communities in which Christianity found root. Judge shows the importance for the wider Roman culture and for the Christian groups that arose within that culture of such basic social perceptions as *politeia* (citizenship), *oikonomia* (household identity), and *koinonia* (community; shared experience and identity). He concludes that these Christian groups in such places as Corinth were not the proletariat, but "were dominated by a socially pretentious section of the population of the big cities" (60). In all probability, the members of these Christian communities were more varied than Judge's reconstruction allows for, and he leaves out of consideration entirely the issues of leadership within these groups. A major drawback in his approach is his failure to discriminate between the social contexts of the authentic Pauline letters, of the stories in Acts, and of the later material attributed to Paul. Acts fits Judge's hypothesis, but Paul's own letters and the deutero-Pauline material present more complex situations socially and culturally than Judge allows for.

A similar handicap besets an otherwise important and useful study by Derek Tidball, *The Social Context of the New Testament*.[17] His summaries and assessments of social theories as they have been employed for analysis of the New Testament are on the whole accurate and judicious, especially his discussions of the early church as sect and the social status of the early Christians. But his use of all the Pauline material (the authentic letters, Acts, and the Pastorals) on the same level precludes his discerning the social, cultural, and conceptual changes that are reflected in this spectrum of sources about and attributed to Paul.

Missing from nearly all these studies is adequate attention to the factors in the origins of Christianity which are illuminated by social theoreticians who deal with the dynamics of group formation and change, and the emergence and modification of leadership roles within these religious groups. To studies that treat these factors we now turn.

Social Dynamics and Social Roles

The profound and enduring impact of sociology on the study of religion in terms of development of religious movements and the changing leadership roles is evident in the work of two scholars from the early part of this century: Emile Durkheim and Max Weber. Durkheim noted the collective nature of religious thought, ritual, and group identity: they are "social affairs and the product of collective thought." Or again, "The really religious beliefs are always common to a determined [i.e., limited] group, which makes profession of adhering to them and of practicing rites connected with them. They are not merely received individually by the members of the group; they are something belonging to a group, and they make its unity."[18] Durkheim's observations warn against sharp differentiations between the social group and its shared commitments and practices. It is not enough to examine sociologically either the rites and doctrines of a group or the social structures that it embodies: both must be analyzed in relation to each other for accurate understanding.

Max Weber's contribution to sociology is enormous, especially to sociology of religion. In the course of his vast studies of various religious traditions, Weber advanced methodological proposals which have had—justifiably—an enduring impact on the field of the study of religion. Two of these are analytical principles which he defined; another of his major insights is a basic pattern of social dynamics in religious movements in general. The first principle is a fundamental distinction between social causality as (1) a function of social-scientific "laws" and (2) as the product of concrete relationships—a distinction that should serve as an enduring warning against the tendency of many sociologists (and biblical scholars influenced by them) to "explain" religious developments by discerning the effects of social laws or by classifying phenomena in fixed categories. Weber wrote, "Where the individuality of a phenomenon is concerned, the question of causality is not a question of *laws* but of concrete *relationship*; it is not a question of the subsumption of the event under some general rubric as a representative case but of its imputation as a consequence of some constellation. Wherever the causal explanation of a 'cultural phenomenon' is under consideration, the knowledge of causal laws is not the *end* of the investigation but only a *means*."[19]

The second basic principle in Weber's work is the *ideal type*. This is "a conceptual construct which is neither a historical reality nor even the 'true' reality. . . . It has the significance of a purely ideal *limiting* concept with which the real situation or action is compared and surveyed for the explication of certain of its significant components. [The function of] the ideal type is an attempt to analyze historically unique configurations of their individual components by means of genetic concepts." Weber warns against identifying reality with the types or using the types as procrustean beds into which historical phenomena are forced: "The goal of ideal-typical construction is always to make clearly explicit, not the class or average character, but rather the unique individual character of cultural phenomena."[20]

The basic pattern that Weber discerned in the development of religious movements was the shift from charismatic origins to institutional forms. In contrast to the routine nature of bureaucratic and patriarchal structures, which are "fashioned to meet calculable and recurrent needs by a normal routine," there arise charismatic leaders in times of psychic, physical, economic, ethical, religious, or political distress. Though they lack special training or authorization by institutional officials, their gifts of body and spirit are seen by at least some of their contemporaries to be rare and supernatural in origin. The leadership of such a movement, which is launched by a prophet or savior figure, soon passes to his charismatically qualified successors, pupils, disciples, and ultimately takes on the form of a hierocracy. Thus the charismatic novelty and the traditionalism stand almost from the outset in tension with each other. Frequently the next generation will reinterpret the promises and principles in a fundamental way, adapting them to the community's new situation following the passing of the academic leader(s).[21]

Weber's work has over the past twenty years inspired a huge amount of analytical literature, much of it focused on the implications of his work for historical study. The most discerning, comprehensive, and nuanced analysis of Weber and the implications of his work for social understanding is that of Susan Hekman.[22] She sets Weber's work against the background of developments in linguistic philosophy (Wittgenstein), of theory concerning method in the natural sciences (Kuhn), as well as of epistemological studies (Habermas and Toulmin). Building on Kuhn's use of Weber,[23] she asserts that in the choice of method and the evaluation of evidence there are always psychological and sociological factors, as well as a value system and institutional structures through which the system of analysis that is chosen is transmitted and reinforced. The result is that there are both subjective and objective factors operative in the choice of an analytical theory: the former are the function of the analyst, given her or his personal and social context; the latter are subject to criticism on the grounds of accuracy, consistency, breadth of scope, simplicity, and fruitfulness as to the results that the method produces.[24]

One of the pioneering essays in the use of Weber's insights about charismatic leadership in emergent religious movements is by Gerd Theissen; it is known in North America as *The Sociology of Early Palestinian Christianity*.[25] Here Theissen shows the charismatic factor operative in both Jesus' own formative role for the Christian movement and in that of the roles assigned by him to the disciples, according to the gospel tradition. It is regrettable, however, that Theissen concentrates mainly on the charismatic roles of Jesus and the disciples as represented in the synoptic tradition, and has only minimal interest in the crucial factors of modes of community leadership and group formation. Both of these factors were, of course, central for the preservation, transmission, and modification of the Jesus movement. Theissen has also examined the social tensions and patterns operative in the Pauline churches—specifically in the church at Corinth—in *The Social Setting of Pauline Christianity*.[26] Here he takes the leadership and organizational aspects more fully into account. These works have had a pervasive and enduring effect on the approach to historical reconstruction of the origins of Christianity.

In addition to the sociological theorists already mentioned, there are a number whose writings have the potential of contributing significantly to analysis of the history and literature of early Christianity, including those that treat of models and patterns in social groups. Here the range is almost limitless, but the following may be noted as having direct importance for this task.

For basic orientation in contemporary sociological theory, a useful, comprehensive critical survey may be found in Jonathan H. Turner, *The Structure of Sociological Theory*.[27] Turner describes and criticizes four basic theories: (1) *functional theory*, which treats society as a functioning organism, with attention to parts and the whole, and to normal and pathological conditions; (2) *conflict theory*, which treats society as a process of events leading to conflict with varying degrees of violence, and some form of conflict resolution; (3) *exchange* or *network theory*, which primarily focuses on the nature of the relationships and exchanges between members of the society or subgroups within it; (4) *interaction theory*, which analyzes the individuals and the microprocesses by which they come to terms with each other in a variety of contexts.

More directly relevant to the analysis of the tensions and changes within early Christianity, as it defines itself over against the various Jewish options of the first century and then struggles to formulate and organize itself in the midst of Roman society, are studies of social differentiation and stratification. Two works that are notably useful for this mode of analysis are those by S. N. Eisenstadt and Gerhard E. Lenski.[28] Among the features of social stratification (in terms of which one finds a place in society) described by Eisenstadt which are directly relevant to Christian origins are the processes of (1) setting criteria for evaluating and legitimating different life-styles, and (2) establishing social identities, regulating access to positions of authority, upholding the approved life-style, and inculcating basic attitudes through some mode of socialization (84).

Among the various types of society described by Lenski, the

one that fits astonishingly well the social, economic, and political conditions of first-century Palestine is that of the "Agrarian Societies." He describes the following features as characteristic of this type of society as opposed to simple horticultural societies. The agrarian society has developed advanced technology and production, and maintains order by means of a strong military structure. The central government controls huge areas with large populations. If governmental pressure is eased, revolts break out. The socially dominant groups, which are in the urban areas, are comprised of officials, priests, scholars, scribes, merchants, servants, soldiers, and craft-workers. They are surrounded by a fringe of beggars and day laborers. The tiny leisure class derives its income from rents, pensions, profits, or political office. The political elite depend on the priestly class to establish and maintain the legitimacy of their rule, to justify their taking from the masses, and to perform low-level administrative, diplomatic, and instructional tasks. The power elite cooperate with the priestly group by building splendid temples and shrines to enhance the government's claim to legitimate domination. The struggles that emerge within the society are often aimed not at overthrow, but at gaining partisan advantage over others. On the bottom of this social structure are the peasants, on whom falls the burden of supporting the state and the economy. From their number emerges a small merchant class that operates the market, in cooperation with the official and client group that serves the lower administrative functions. Together with the artisan class, which serves the merchant class, they are socially, geographically, and economically mobile. They tend to avoid political involvement, since governmental stability helps to assure a steady market for goods and services. These categories, once defined, are immediately appropriate for increasing our understanding of the social, cultural, economic, and political tensions evident in the context in which the Jesus movement began in first-century Palestine, as well as in the wider—predominantly urban—setting in which the Christian movement took hold across the Mediterranean world.

Anthony Saldarini, in *Pharisees, Scribes and Sadducees in Palestinian Society: A Sociological Approach* (Wilmington, Del.: Michael Glazier, 1988), has demonstrated effectively the insights that these sociological methods of Eisenstadt and Lenski provide for understanding the roles of these three important groups in Jewish society. Most studies of these segments of Judaism comment only on their alleged theological differences, or in the case of the scribes and

Pharisees, treat them as equivalents of the rabbis of the second and subsequent centuries. Through Saldarini's use of these analytical approaches one can see the social role that these types of Jewish leaders fulfilled, and hence understand more fully the tensions between them and Jesus that are reflected in the gospels.

Important for assessment of the tensions between the followers of Jesus and the Jewish religious authorities—both during and subsequent to Jesus' career—is the analysis of group conflict by sociologists. Louis Kriesberg notes that not all parties in such conflicts are aware of the issues, which typically involve the undefined but potent factor of collective identity.[29] At stake at the conscious level are such features as the loss of power to another group, the wider social and political conditions in which the conflict emerged, and the perceived relationships among the parties in conflict. Louis Coser treats social, political, and religious conflict.[30] He sides with Weber (against Durkheim) on the theoretical base that social conflict is not pathological but inherent in society. As a result, religion is not merely a cohesive, integrating, and euphoric social force. He quotes, with approval, Robert Merton's observation that the rebel, revolutionary, nonconformist, heretic, or renegade of an earlier epoch may well become the cultural hero of a later day (132). Once again, the import of these factors and the importance of raising them to the level of consciousness for the scholar analyzing the origins of Christianity and its break with Judaism are obvious.

Two important works in which sociological theory has been utilized in order to better understand the formation of leadership roles within the early church are those by John H. Schuetz and Bengt Holmberg.[31] Building on insights from Talcott Parson's *The Structure of Social Action,*[32] Schuetz shows that the issue of the legitimacy of Paul's apostolic role rests on his claim to moral authority for his position which derives from his having been divinely commissioned for his task and instructed for the interpretation of the divine message to the human race (18-20). The gospel that Paul preaches provides the warrant for his apostolic role. Paul does not define his authority, and where the problem arises, he leaves it unresolved, appealing only to his commissioning by God (181).

Holmberg explicitly limits his inquiry to the historical study of the structure of authority in the primitive church as evident in the letters of Paul. He eschews theological discussion in favor of seeking out what is *assumed* in these documents, as distinct from what is directly stated. His method derives from social anthropology. Accordingly, he culls from the letters data on the distribution of power in the early church: (1) power within the churches of the Pauline region; (2) power within the local Pauline churches, including such roles as apostle, prophet, teacher, administrator; (3) Paul's own charismatic authority; (4) the institutionalization of charismatic authority; and (5) the institutionalization in the primitive church. The brilliant work of Holmberg concludes with an appeal to move beyond merely tracing conceptual development of the external features of institutional change to look at the social factors that underlie and help to shape both these modes of transformation within the early church.

Holmberg's agenda has a precedent among sociologists: several have set themselves precisely to the task of examining ancient culture with reference to the sociological models. A clear detailing of the types of models and the analytical processes for using them is that by T. F. Carney.[33] Another broad study of religious phenomena that proceeds by describing types of religious culture and the patterns of change that they undergo is the one by Roland Robertson.[34] The most direct links between sociological methods and analysis of evidence in religious history, however, are in the field of cultural anthropology, the focus of the next section of this survey.

Anthropological Analysis and Group Identity

Chapter 1 cited briefly the contribution of anthropologists to the study of Christian origins. It is important to indicate in more specific ways, however, how their methods directly illuminate aspects of the early Christian movement and its literature.

Basic to the anthropological approach to the study of religion as a social phenomenon is the observation of Emile Durkheim: "Religious representations are collective representations which express collective realities; the rites are a manner of acting which takes rise in the midst of the assembled groups and which are destined to excite, maintain or re-create certain mental states in these groups. So if the categories are of religious origin, they ought to participate in this nature common to all religious facts; they too should be social affairs and the product of collective thought."[35]

The bearing of this understanding of religion as a phenomenon requiring analysis by sociological modes is linked with the task of the historian by E. E. Evans-Pritchard, in an essay, "Anthropology and History,"[36] where he asserts that there is only a technical, not a methodological, difference between social anthropology and history. In contrast with narrative historians or philosophers of history, he notes especially the work of social historians as kindred to that of the anthropologists, since they "are interested in social institutions, in mass movements and great cultural changes." They seek to discern "regularities, tendencies, types and typical sequences . . . always within a restricted historical and cultural context" (174). "Both historians and anthropologists are fully aware that any event has the character of uniqueness and generality, and that in an interpretation of it both [factors] have to be given consideration" (175). He reverses the dictum of F. W. Maitland[37] that "anthropology must choose between being history and being nothing," by asserting, "History must choose between being social anthropology and being nothing" (190).

Lucy Mair has developed this approach in a wide-ranging work,[38] in which she deals with religions and their historical developments, including such features as ritual, morals, magic, leadership roles, and myth. Using myth in the sense of explanations that arise concerning the "why" of the cosmos and human existence—as distinct from the "how" raised by scientists—Mair concludes that myths arise when people seek for unifying principles beneath the diversity of experience, just as scientists use theoretical models to understand the processes of the universe (257). Her work implicitly invites New Testament scholars to examine the relationship between mythic elements in the early Christian writings and the shape and intentions of the various communities which in their diversity comprised the early Christian movement.

By far the most direct and substantive contribution to a demonstration of the links between anthropology and the study of religion is that of Clifford Geertz.[39] His definition of religion encompasses five major points. Religion is [1] a system of symbols which acts to [2] establish powerful, persuasive, and long-lasting human moods and motivations by [3] formulating conceptions of a general order of existence and [4] clothing these conceptions with such an aura of factuality that [5] the moods and motivations seem uniquely realistic. By symbol, Geertz means models of linguistic, graphic, mechanical, and natural processes which function not to provide sources of information in terms of which other processes can be patterned, but to represent those patterned processes as such—to express their structure in an alternative medium. This program, whether taken as representational or conceptual, is "the essence of human thought" (94). What religion does is to imbue such a system of symbols with a persuasive authority (112).

Like Weber, Geertz warns against mislabeling the results of

cultural analysis by setting forth "symmetrical crystals of significance, purified of the material complexity in which they are located," and then attributing "their existence to autogenous principles of order, universal properties of the human mind, or vast, *a priori Weltanschauungen.*" To do so is "to pretend a science that does not exist and to pretend a reality that cannot be found" (20). Here, of course, the charge offered by Geertz fits well the scholarly approach of the history-of-religions school. Rather than adopting this so-called objective approach, the analyst of culture, including religion, must maintain a balance between the discernment of patterns of perception that are shared by several cultures and the features which are distinctive to the cultural phenomena under present scrutiny. Central features of religions are ethos (the approved style of life) and worldview (the assumed structure of reality). "Religion, by fusing ethos and worldview, gives to a set of social values what they perhaps most need to be coercive: an appearance of objectivity. In sacred rituals and myths, values are portrayed, not as subjective human preferences, but as the imposed conditions for life implicit in a world with a particular structure" (131). Responsible analysis of a religious tradition—including that of early Christianity in its various stages and forms—must take into account these components, to which Geertz draws attention in their interrelationships: myths, symbols, ritual, ethos, structure, group identity.

From Geertz's insights New Testament scholars must learn that historical inquiry in this field should avoid simple identification of features of early Christianity which resemble elements in Greco-Roman culture, but must instead examine the details in relation to the whole symbolic system. It is not sufficient, for example, to note the superficial similarity between Jesus, who dies and rises again according to the Christian tradition, and Osiris, who dies and rises annually, in consonance with the annual rise and fall of the Nile. Geertz correctly notes the interrelationships among the moral and evaluative aspects of a culture, the overall view of reality shared by the society, and the meanings which he says are "stored" in such symbols as the cross.[40] It is the dynamic configuration of these factors that must be taken into account, rather than merely classification of items on the basis of apparent similarity with features of culture and religion in the Greco-Roman world.

A perceptive and useful schematic approach to the role of religion in personal identity is that of Hans J. Mol.[41] His thesis is that what constitutes the sacred develops as a result of one's projecting an order that is beyond the contradictions and contingencies of life as experienced (*objectification*). That order evokes a personal *commitment*, which is confirmed through stylized actions (*ritual*) and depicted in terms of a sacred story (*myth*). By these interrelated modes of understanding, persons find a common identity, which provides them with a sense of place and purpose in the cosmos. This process is akin to the theory basic to sociology of knowledge, as we shall note below. Mol's extensive writings document this configuration of factors that provide the basis for personal identity. Here again there is the call from outside the field of New Testament studies to use an integrative approach to historical analysis which will make possible the understanding of the relationships between such seemingly diverse features of the New Testament as the thought-world of the time, the experience of conversion, the creation and adaptation of ritual modes by the early Christians, and the stories of God's work among them through Jesus and the apostles.

One specific area of research by anthropologists which has a direct link with the origins of Christianity is the study of the beginnings and the development of millennarian groups. Among the earlier studies of the dynamics and social factors conducive to the arise of millennarian sects are those by Leon Festinger et al.,[42] Norman Cohn,[43] Peter Worsley,[44] Kenelm Burridge,[45] and Bryan Wilson.[46] These studies examine the phenomenon of religious groups in America and in Third World cultures which expect some form of divine intervention that will bring to an end the present age or order and establish a divine rule. The implications of these studies for the historical analysis of early Christianity have been explored by John Gager[47] and, with particular reference to the apocalyptic orientation of the Gospel of Mark, by me.[48]

The factors that give rise to such movements are conveniently summarized by Burridge: Out of a sense of oppression and powerlessness, a group perceives a redemptive process at work, by which the structure of power and of moral obligation is being transformed (or a transformation is promised). The chosen group has been given insight concerning this renewal and guidelines for individual and common life in the new society. These perceptions have been disclosed through a prophetic figure, who provides the answers to the group's questions and serves as the model for its hopes and behavior. It is easy to see the similarities between the descriptions of modern millennarian groups and the origins of

Christianity: the appearance of Jesus, who announces the impending end of the age; his claim to be the agent of God in preparing others to share in the New Age; his sharing these insights with his faithful followers; and the adjustment that the Jesus movement must make when the end does not come at the expected time. This factor of nonfulfillment was of major importance for the early Christians during and subsequent to the New Testament period. Studies of millennarian groups show that such movements characteristically make adjustments when their initial expectations are not fulfilled. Sociologically speaking, the early Christian problem about the delay of the *parousia* of Jesus is by no means unique.

Recently, as we noted in chapter 1, considerable attention has been given to the import of the self-definition of religious communities as perceived and analyzed by the anthropologist Mary Douglas in her earlier works, and further refined in her more recent publications. In *Purity and Danger,*[49] Douglas observes that "defilement is never an isolated event. It cannot occur except in view of a systematic ordering of ideas. . . . The only way in which pollution ideas make sense is in reference to a total structure of thought whose keystone, boundaries, margins and internal lines are held in relation by rituals of separation" (41). The central concern is for holiness, which is an attribute of the godhead and which is the means of creating order through which human affairs may prosper. It includes wholeness and completeness, so that those who fail to meet this requirement are excluded. It is unity, integrity, perfection of the individual and the kind (49-52). In the tradition of ancient Israel, the injunction to inscribe the law on the heart, on the frontlets between the eyes, and on the doorposts shows that these are the ground of the ordered life in the divinely ordered cosmos (57). What is created in cleansing and purifying is "a total universe in which all experience is ordered." These insights shed light on the controversy evident in the New Testament between Jesus and his followers, on the one hand, and the Pharisees, on the other, over the issue of the Christians' nonobservance of the Jewish purity laws. What is involved is not merely details about ritual, but the larger question of conflicting modes of community definition.

In another basic contribution to anthropological analysis of societies,[50] Douglas wrote, "There is no person whose life does not need to unfold in a coherent symbolic system." Both social responsibility and social organization are dependent on a symbol system. To draw the lines and boundaries of such a system is a way of ordering experience, of creating the basis for human relationships, and for enabling persons to realize ultimate meaning (72). Douglas developed a scheme for differentiating these symbolic universes, which she calls Group/Grid. We have seen that Douglas, by measuring a society's complexity (grid) in relation to the degree to which it controls its members (group), derives four cosmological types (see chap. 1, p. 16, above). Thus she provides a typology for discerning the range in the degree to which a society develops an extensive and articulate system in defining its place in the universe. Group is her index of the degree to which the society's symbols and values control the lives of its members. We have seen how she differentiates four cosmological types, according to this scheme:

1. low grid/low group: individualism
2. high grid/low group: a complex society in which roles are assigned and accepted
3. low grid/high group: factionalism, in which only the external boundary is clear; all other statuses are open and subject to negotiation
4. high grid/high group: an institution where hierarchy is respected and loyalty is rewarded.

She sees this analytical method as providing a typology for discerning the range of ways in which "alternative visions of society are selected and sustained."[51] In each case, there is an implicit cosmology that comprises the ultimate justifying ideas that are invoked or assumed as if part of the natural order. Again, they are not at all natural; they emerge from social interaction.[52] Douglas extends the famous dictum of Durkheim, "Society is God," to mean that in every culture the image of society is endowed with sacredness and the idea of God is correlated with the idea of the society.

Since the biblical writings are characteristically concerned with the range and change of understanding concerning the relationship of God with his people, the Group/Grid analytical scheme is valuable as a mode of interpretation and an instrument for discerning historical distinctions within the biblical period. Douglas presents her scheme as "a few grand types, each of which generates necessarily its own self-sustaining perceptual blinkers."[53] Thus her methodological proposal functions in ways that resemble Weber's ideal types. She does not establish categories into which phenomena are to be classified, but catalytic agents to heighten an interpreter's sensitivity as to certain features of one group which are

Sociological Approaches

shared with others, while acknowledging the distinctive features of this exemplary "type," as well. This essential perception about group identity and definition has not always been taken into account by those seeking to utilize sociological—and specifically anthropological—insights for historical understanding of Christian origins.[54]

An important contribution to our understanding of how such sociological factors were at work in the formulation of various types of community in the early Christian movement is John H. Elliott's study of the conditions in the northern provinces of Asia Minor which shaped the life of the community represented in 1 Peter.[55] Although the time and the circumstances are significantly different for the origins of the Gospel of Mark, methods similar to Elliott's are used in the definition and description of the community apparent in and behind that Gospel in my own work on Mark.[56]

Among those scholars who have employed methods and insights from sociological studies of conflict within peasant societies, Richard A. Horsley and John S. Hanson have produced a fresh and revealing analysis of the evidence from Josephus and the New Testament about those groups that were a challenge to the social and political stability of Palestine in the first century.[57] Their work builds especially on the insights of Eric Hobsbawm's study of social banditry in peasant societies.[58] They show that the threat to the Roman-imposed order in Palestine was not from insurrectionists (until the 60s), but from impoverished peasants who turned to banditry as a means of survival in a sociopolitical state dominated by and run for the benefit of a tiny elite and their clients. It is along similar lines of sociological analysis that Anthony Saldarini has written his study of the social class of the Pharisees in the first century.[59]

Among the studies that are concerned with the social identity of the members of the various early Christian groups, three are representative. The first is by Ronald F. Hock,[60] who builds on the indications in the letters about Paul's self-employment as an artisan (Acts 18:3 specifies tent-making). Hock seeks to show the links in attitude and propaganda strategy between the apostle to the Gentiles and the practices of Cynic philosophers. He considers but dismisses the notion that Paul, like the later rabbis, combined a trade with the study and teaching of Torah. Hock's study illumines the financial dimensions of the early churches, and sheds light on otherwise puzzling aspects of Paul's understanding of his apostolic role.

49

Several recent publications treat the social factor of community participation. John Koenig, for instance, describes the attitude of Jesus toward those considered to be religious and moral outsiders by first-century standards of Jewish piety.[61] He seeks to show that this social dimension of the early Christian movement was an important factor in its wide appeal and rapid spread. He details this dimension of the movement in relation to Jesus, as portrayed in the older gospel tradition, to Paul, and to the writings of Luke. J. Paul Sampley traces the similarities and differences between the Roman concept of *societas* and the Pauline notion of *koinonia,* as it is expounded and detailed in Paul's Letters to the Corinthians, to the Philippians, and to Philemon.[62] The indications that the Christian communities transcended religious, social, economic, and sexual barriers in the dominant society of the time—both Jewish and Greco-Roman—are thus seen to be factors that are not merely theologically appealing, but of enduring significance in the expansion of the church.

Sociology of Knowledge

Alfred Schutz, whose education in Germany brought him under the influence of Max Weber and Edmund Husserl, on migrating to America in 1939 was deeply affected by the pragmatic, humanistic theories of John Dewey and William James. Out of this matrix emerged his view of knowledge as a sociological construction:[63] "The world of daily life is the organized world, the intersubjective world," which is experienced and interpreted by others, our predecessors, and which we have to modify by our actions or that will modify our actions. Each person is in a "biographically determined situation," which provides his or her space, role, status, and moral or ideological position. It has a history, a sedimentation of all previous human experiences, and especially of those perceived and experienced within the society in which the individual resides (72-73). These features of the socially constructed understanding of the world do not determine in any absolute sense what one thinks or does, but they do predict how one is likely to respond to the world. Those who decide voluntarily to adopt another "knowledge" must learn and appropriate it. Members of the outgroup, however, do not regard the articles of faith and the historical tradition of the ingroup as self-evident, since their own central myths, as well as their process of rationalization and institutionalization are different.

Lacking or refusing to use a translation code, they consider another group's natural attitude—even when it in many ways may overlap with their own—as perverse and hostile. The members of one group may try to educate or convert the benighted—or declare war on them (84-85). Schutz epitomizes his view of knowledge as social: "The social world into which one is born and within which one has to find his bearings is experienced as a tight-knit web of social relationships, of systems and signs and symbols with their particular structure of meaning, of institutional forms of social organization, of systems of status and prestige, etc. The meaning of all these elements of the social world in all its diversity and stratification, as well as the pattern of the texture itself, is by those living within it taken for granted" (80).

The implications of this view of knowledge for historical understanding are profound. As Schutz and Thomas Luckmann have stated the case,[64] the transmission of subjective knowledge becomes objectivated and socialized in signs, which process leads to idealization and anonymization. They mean by this that what is initially perceived as personal knowledge comes to be expressed in general terms that are assumed to be universally recognized as valid by all members of the society ("Everyone knows that . . ."). But this leads to the articulation of that knowledge in general, impersonal terms, which are treated as being universally valid and are stated in abstract formulations, often through the use of shared symbols. This symbolized knowledge can preserve either the specific authority of a legendary or historical knowledge, or the anonymous authority of the "forefathers" (e.g., "everyone"). "It is thus . . . that knowledge comes to have an overwhelming and at the same time taken-for-granted independence, which in the end is based on the subjective results of experience and explication, but which contrasts with the individual and the subjectivity of his experience and situation. It need hardly be said that the social validity of such 'objectivated' knowledge can outlast its original social relevance" (284). The socially accepted symbol system may be altered under the impact of individual or corporate experience, or a typical new knowledge may lead to a change in the system of signs or to its replacement by a new system (285).

It is clear that this kind of reappraisal of the older signs-system is in process in first-century Judaism, as well as in early Christianity, and that the outcomes include reconstitution as well as radical replacement of the signs within both Judaism and early Christianity.

For example, Wisdom, which in Proverbs 8 is pictured as a companion or co-worker with God as the world was being created, is portrayed in Wisdom of Solomon in language borrowed from Greek philosophy as the eternal principle of order and as the instrument of disclosure of the divine nature (Wisdom of Solomon 7). In early Christianity, the role of Wisdom is taken over by the Greek synonym, *logos*, with the result that Jesus is presented in John 1 as both the instrument of creation and of divine self-disclosure.

As we noted earlier (chap. 1) Peter Berger has made important refinements in the analysis of sociology of knowledge, including his definition of *externalization* (the shaping of culture and society by language, symbols, institutions, laws); *internalization* (the subjective identification of the self with the social world); and *socialization* (the transmission by society of its meaning to the new generation and its effort to conform that generation to social standards and institutions.[65]

The relevance of this pattern of social appropriation for the New Testament is clear. In the Gospel of Mark, for example, Jesus is portrayed as the agent of God, in the prophetic tradition of Israel, through whom God's rule is about to become effective in the created world. His words and works provide the norms for what the new community is supposed to do to prepare for this event, and his death and resurrection are the basic symbols for the renewal of the covenant. To the extent that his followers commit themselves to this understanding, it becomes the motivation for their lives. And as a group they have a new mode of social identity, which they pass on by preaching and teaching.

Berger,[66] along with Thomas Luckmann, describes the nomic role of the symbolic universe constructed and affirmed by the society, which "provides powerful legitimation for the institutional order as a whole as well as for particular sectors of it," including the history of the culture. The symbol system "locates all collective events in a cohesive unity that includes past, present and future" so that the empirical community is transposed to a cosmic plane.[67]

An essential feature of the process of world-construction, as Berger describes it, is what he calls *legitimation*. This is the process, which begins at the intuitive level and moves in stages to the explicit level, by which the structure of reality as perceived by the group is objectified, affirmed, and justified. Its first stage is pre-theoretical, when the community names institutions or practices and thereby begins the process of legitimating them. The second stage is that of primitive theoretical legitimation in the form of proverbs and aphoristic sayings that are assumed to be self-evidently true. The third stage involves direct theoretical legitimation in relation to specific institutional and conceptual aspects of the culture. The fourth and final stage is the integration of the various provinces of practice and meaning into a symbolic totality. Careful analysis of the writings of early Christianity reveal various stages in this legitimation process.[68] One can see this process at work as one moves from the Gospel of Mark, with its largely undefined roles for the disciples, the lack of any clear plan for the spread of the gospel, and the indefiniteness of the expectation of the time of the coming of the New Age, to the Gospel of Matthew, where the role of the disciples is specified (Matthew 16), the plan for settling disagreements within the community is offered (Matthew 18), and the forms and modes of worldwide outreach for the gospel are given (Matthew 28).

The historian, therefore, cannot rest content with the social description of such phenomena as economic factors, archeological remains, social patterns, institutional forms, or even literary evidence in and of itself. Rather, the historian must seek to enter into the symbolic universe of the community that produced this evidence, and to identify both what the shared assumptions were as well as what explicit claims and norms were declared by the group. Unless this analytical approach is undertaken, it is virtually certain that the unconscious assumptions and values of the interpreter will be imposed on the ancient evidence. Perhaps that fault is not wholly to be avoided, but the approach defined by sociology of knowledge is an essential safeguard against guileless cultural imperialism on the part of the interpreter of another time and culture.

The growing recognition by sociologists of the validity and potential of this approach is evident in the collection of critical essays by Robert Wuthnow and others on the theoretical work of Berger, Mary Douglas, Michel Foucault, and Juergen Habermas.[69] In his essay on Berger, Wuthnow examines and supports Berger's approach to the analysis of cultures, both contemporary and ancient. Mary Douglas, while critical of some of the details of Berger's approach, by the very title of her book, shows kinship with and support for the basic enterprise, which seeks to develop an encompassing typology for discovering "how alternative visions of society are selected and sustained."[70] In examining a culture, she seeks to identify the implicit cosmology which constitutes "the ultimate justifying ideas which tend to be invoked as if part of the natural order and yet which . . . are not at all natural but strictly a product of social interaction." As she phrases it paradoxically, "There is nothing natural about the perception of nature" (5). Since Mary Douglas's analytical work ranges freely from ancient to modern cultures, the methodological significance of identifying the shared perceptions of a culture is as important for the historian as it is for the cultural anthropologist.

In my own historical work, I have sought to employ the insights and methods of sociology of knowledge—without discounting the contribution of social description, analysis of social dynamics in relation to leadership and group formation, and of social anthropology with its examination of group identity. In 1980 I offered an exploratory essay along these lines.[71] A more recent statement on and demonstration of the significance of sociological methods for historical understanding appeared in my work on miracles.[72] Additional evidence of the method is offered in my work on *Medicine, Miracle, and Magic in New Testament Times*.[73] In the two latter works, I seek to show that healing is a phenomenon which has to be understood in terms of the specific context in which it is reported as occurring. Just because there is a famous third-century C.E. account of an itinerant wonder-working philosopher, in Philostratus's *Life of Apollonius of Tyana*, there is no warrant for the assumption by scholars in the history-of-religions school tradition that the early Christians who were recounting in the Gospels the miracles of Jesus were doing so by modeling him after Apollonius. Instead, there is evidence that in the Jewish apocalyptic tradition, with which Jesus' message shows obvious kinship, miracles were seen as a sign of divine action in behalf of beleaguered people. And that is precisely how Jesus is portrayed as explaining the meaning of his exorcisms and healings. Context, not category, is once more the essential clue to historical interpretation.

Two recent works which draw on the insights of Peter Berger, and especially on his concept of "legitimation" to account for the distinctive forms of early Christianity to be found within the New Testament are Philip S. Esler's *Community and Gospel in Luke Acts: The Social and Political Motivations of Lucan Theory* (Cambridge and New York: Cambridge University Press, 1988) and J. Andrew Overman's forthcoming *Matthew's Gospel and Formative Judaism: A Study in the Social World of the Matthew Community* (forthcoming from Fortress Press). By use of Berger's theory of legitimation both these writers help to account for the re-working of the gospel material in each of these gospels, and to illuminate the attitudes toward

Judaism, the Roman state, and toward the emergent leadership structures within the church.

Linguistics, Epistemology, and Hermeneutics

In contrast to modes of linguistic analysis which limit their range of inquiry to grammar, syntax, and interlingual functions, the field of sociolinguistics is concerned with the social context in which linguistic communication occurs and develops. For example, William Labov asserts that "one cannot understand the development of language change apart from the social life of the community in which it occurs."[74]

Dell Hymes declares that in the study of language, "one cannot take form, a given code, or even speech itself as a limiting frame of reference. One must take as context a community or network of persons, investigating its communicative activities as a whole. . . ." Elements that constitute the communicative economy of a group are "the boundaries of the community . . . the means and purposes and patterns of selection [chosen by the community], their structure and hierarchy." The same linguistic means may be made to serve various ends. The same communicative ends may be served linguistically by various means. "Facets of the cultural values and beliefs, social institutions and forms, roles and personalities, history and ecology of a community may have to be examined in their bearing on communicative events and patterns."[75]

In *Language and Social Networks*, Lesley Milroy warns against identifying a linguistic group by "social class." He prefers the term "community," since it points to the social network that manifests the interrelations between the language in its distinctive features and those who speak it.[76] Additionally, language as a primary ground of social identity is explored and analyzed by John J. Gumperz,[77] and by R. B. LePage and Andree Tabouret-Keller.[78] Although each of these writers is treating language in relation to contemporary communities, the factors that are essential to their analysis are the symbolic worlds shared by the members of the linguistic community under study.

The relevance of these studies for the interpretation of the New Testament is direct. Both the various forms of Judaism out of which the Christian communities developed and the diverse forms that the Christian communities took—in their formative stages and as they developed in successive generations—are reflected in their respective linguistic usages. Scholars have been content to build theories on terminology and literary forms shared by these groups, without taking into account the transforming effect of the community and its life-world, which has employed these superficially similar patterns of thought and expression. It is attention to such factors of transformation for which sociolinguists are calling. In spite of the learned and informative character of Gerhard Kittel's *Theological Dictionary of the New Testament,*[79] it is lacking in this nuanced approach to the specific linguistic and symbolic meanings of the New Testament words in the specific sociocultural contexts in which they are used.

The importance of the sociolinguistic mode of analysis has been highlighted by the work of Bible translation, especially through the pioneering research and translation activity of Eugene Nida. In one of his earlier works,[80] he discussed the semantic context of a statement: the range of situations in which lexical symbols appear, and the paralinguistic features of language (voice, pitch, rhythm, tempo) used by the speaker. Nida also noted the three types of meaning: (1) situational vs. behavioral meanings (the interplay between the circumstances and the reactions of the participants); (2) linguistic vs. extralinguistic meanings (such as the paralinguistic features just mentioned); and (3) cognitive vs. somatic meanings (the dynamic between the dictionary definitions of words and the bodily reactions to them on the part of the users or hearers). These are theoretically distinguishable, but are in fact mingled in concrete situations (41). The responsibility of the translator, therefore, is to take into account these dimensions of the document to be translated, and on that basis: (1) reduce the source text to its structurally simplest and most semantically evident kernels; (2) transfer the meaning from the source language to the receptor language on a structurally simple level; and (3) generate the stylistically and semantically equivalent expression in the receptor language (68), that is, the language of the hearers or readers of the translation.

In his more recent writings, Nida becomes even more explicit about the profound effect on meaning that derives from the social orientation and shared worldview of the linguistic user. The technical linguistic terms used by Nida may be defined as follows:

> *Morphology:* such formal features of a language as number, person, tense, mode, gender, voice.
> *Semantic structure:* the pattern of meaning of the words used in a sentence.

Syntactic structure: the style in terms of which the words of a statement are arranged in order to convey the intended meaning.

Phonology: the ways that the words of a statement sound or are received by the hearer or reader, in terms of the actual alphabetical sounds of the language.

Unlike morphological or syntactical structures of language, which change very slowly, "the semantic structure may undergo significant changes in a relatively short time, especially within the area of cultural focus. . . . Any ideological system may transform a word so that it is almost unrecognizable." He goes on to show that the semantic structure "reveals more clearly than any other part of language a people's worldview," although it is not apparent from the purely formal structures of the language but must be inferred from a range of clues.[81] Ideally, the translator would have access to all the background that the original writer and his audience shared (184), but the effort must be made to reconstruct it as fully and sensitively as the evidence allows.

More recently,[82] Nida has offered the following counsel for the procedures involved in translation and interpretation: "One must study first the phonological, lexical, syntactical and rhetorical features of the text, and on the basis of these three attempt to determine what are likely to have been the primary [linguistic] functions. Once the functions have been recognized, one can more readily see the ways in which certain strategies have been employed. On the basis of added background information which may be available with regard to a text, one can then recognize some of the reasons for certain decisions made with regard to receptors [hearers and readers] and setting [literary and rhetorical styles], and finally one is likely to arrive at an approximation of the original concept of source, particularly if further information is available concerning the background of the source" (47-48).

The implications of these insights for the study of early Christianity are clear: the interpreter of New Testament texts cannot be content with noting lexical links with other literatures—Jewish or Greco-Roman—or with discerning syntactical or literary patterns analogous to those known from other sources. What is required, beyond these recognitions of surface similarities, is careful assessment of the ideological effects, the implicit assumptions, the larger aims, the underlying world view that is operative in the document

57

under scrutiny. For these purposes, sensitivity to social and cultural factors and forces is indispensable. Thus, for example, one should not impose the same meaning on the term "righteousness" as it is used by Paul and the Gospel of Matthew, since the syntactical frameworks in which each of these writers employs that term differ widely: for Paul it is an action of God—God setting things right—whereas for Matthew it is a quality of behavior which is demanded by God and to be fulfilled by his faithful servants.

A new kind of lexicon has just been published which will make accessible to the interpreter and translator of the New Testament the insights of sociolinguistics sketched herein: *Greek-English Lexicon of the New Testament Based on Semantic Domains.*[83] Its method is to group the vocabulary of the New Testament by categories of meaning, rather than by the traditional dictionary form of the words. There are ninety-three of these "semantic domains," which range from plants, animals, foods, kinship terms, and agriculture, to such abstractions as "nature, class, example," "power, force," "attitudes and emotions." The lexicon invites more subtle and significant comparisons than the traditional approach, which is often arbitrary in implying meanings derived from other allegedly parallel texts. This lexical strategy will help the interpreter to enter into the thought-world of the particular writer whose text is under analysis.

The importance of these sociolinguistic dimensions of inquiry by the interpreter/historian is confirmed by developments in the fields of linguistic philosophy and epistemology. These have been discussed in chapter 1, but some general indications of the dynamics of this social understanding of human knowledge may be offered here. The crucial figure here is Ludwig Wittgenstein. In his earlier *Tractatus Logico-Philosophicus,* he portrayed language on the analogy with pictures as signifiers, but in his later *Philosophical Investigations* he employs the term "language game" as an indication that the speaking of a language is part of an activity and a form of life (23). What determines what is true or false is what people say, not some mode of transcendent logic on which all agree (241). The "game" designation does not intend to trivialize human thought or reduce it to frivolous choices, but to point to the universal human experience of communicating and functioning within a society by a tacitly agreed upon set of rules about meanings and responsibilities. The analyst of human communication cannot be content with recognizing verbal symbols shared by two or more systems of thought. She or he must inquire as to the specific function that the symbols play within that particular language game.

Sociological Approaches

We considered earlier the insightful study by David Bloor on Wittgenstein, in which he notes that the meaning of a word is determined by its use in a particular configuration of shared human understanding. One of his observations has particular relevance for the field of historical inquiry, where—as in so many intellectual endeavors—the ground rules change: "When we detect a change in a language game, we must look for a shift in the goals and purposes of its players which is sufficiently widespread and sufficiently uniform to yield that change. Confronted by competing usages, we should look for rival groups and track down the causes of rivalry; if we see language games merging with one another, we must look for, and try to explain, the continuities and alliances between their players."[84] Bloor's insights are relevant for the changing approaches to historical study in our own times, as well as for the competing claims within Judaism and early Christianity as to divine leadership and covenantal participation.

The hermeneutical implications of Wittgenstein's work have been developed by Hans Gadamer, who, in *Truth and Method*,[85] differentiates the "two horizons": that of the interpreted document and that of the interpreter. As has been observed by Susan Hekman,[86] Gadamer is persuaded that all understanding is linguistic and that understanding in the human sciences is therefore to be examined through the medium of language.

We have also noted (chap. 1) the significance of these insights for biblical interpretation, as spelled out by Anthony Thiselton in *The Two Horizons: Hermeneutics and Philosophical Description*.[87] Gadamer's epistemological and hermeneutical perceptions have profoundly influenced—by shaping insights and issues—Richard J. Bernstein[88] and Susan J. Hekman.[89] Although each of these works has its own distinctive features, they share with such earlier philosophical writings as those by Ian G. Barbour[90] and Nelson Goodman,[91] the recognition that what are called "facts" are not objective, self-existent entities. As Barbour expresses it, "Cultural presuppositions condition all interpretive categories" (55). This is equally the case with scientific and religious knowledge. Or as Bernstein observes, the mode of analysis that a scholar employs involves a choice of theory, which is "a judgmental activity requiring imagination, interpretation, the weighing of alternatives, and application of criteria that are essentially open," a procedure which emphasizes "the role of example and judgmental interpretation" (56-57).

Once again this way of understanding human knowledge has basic implications for the interpretive methods employed by the modern scholar and for the assessment of ancient evidence, which must be regarded as part of a distinctive, complex, symbolic universe rather than as a structure comprised of timeless, objective components to be evaluated in relation to a universal scheme. A case in point for the New Testament interpreter is the difference between Bultmann's proposal that Jesus' message was a model of the timeless call to decision and recent contextual analyses of the Gospels which show the range of ways in which the gospel of Jesus was understood and responded to by the various writers. Unfortunately, some modern literary critics still attempt to find in ancient writings eternal principles or patterns of human experience, while closing their minds to the distinctive nature of the linguistic features of the writers.

Perhaps the most perceptive and potentially fruitful discussion of the hermeneutics which Gadamer has proposed is by Susan Hekman:[92] she denounces the "enlightenment agenda," which tries to develop a social scientific methodology based on the eternal truths of human nature, purged of historical and cultural prejudices, and follows the now discredited nomological-deductive method of the natural sciences in order to formulate scientific truth about human beings. In contrast to this approach, and contingent upon the work of Gadamer, Hekman asserts that what is central in the sociology of knowledge is understanding, not objectivity, with the result that the natural sciences are dependent on the social sciences, not the reverse. Since thought and action are performed by language and tradition, pre-understanding is essential for understanding the social world. What is required for understanding the human social world is a linking of pre-understanding with a critical evaluation of the cultural tradition (155-58).

This method is essential for the interpretation of the range of responses to the figure of Jesus and his message on the part of the various writers within the New Testament, ranging from the apocalyptic outlooks of Mark, Paul, and John (the author of Revelation), to the synthesis of the message of Jesus with the philosophical modes of the epoch, as is evident in James and Hebrews. What Hekman says about the social sciences is fully applicable to the task of the social historian, including the historian of the origins of Christianity.

Structuralism and Deconstructionism

One approach to interpretation of the early Christian documents which considers itself to be informed by the social sciences is that of the structuralists. A defense and a demonstration of this method are offered by François Bovon and others.[93] It is the aim of Bovon to free exegesis from inquiring about the author or thought of a document, focussing instead on the text alone, comprising a total construct, and thereby determining the function of the text (20). An example of this approach is the analysis of Mark 5:1-20 by Jean Starobinski, which consists of (unwitting) allegorical exegesis, in the differentiation of the literary from the spiritual level. The story of Jesus expelling the demons from the tomb-dweller near Gerasa is "no longer an episode of the earthly ministry of Jesus, a moment from his life in time: it is a timeless victory to which each individual is able to appeal for deliverance from his spiritual torment." Starobinski considers it a triumph that by this exegetical approach, "the historicity of the narrative is dissipated" (88). In spite of the claim that structuralist method confronts the text alone, it is obviously an intellectualistic ploy for escaping the text and its context.

In his study on *Paul's Faith and the Power of the Gospel*,[94] Daniel Patte announced a method apparently similar to that of the sociology-of-knowledge, which concentrates on what Paul was assuming, rather than on what he consciously thought he was doing. Behind Paul's faith is a meta-system: a system of convictions which deal with binary oppositions: What is good/evil? What is real/unreal? Patte distinguishes this sharply from Paul's theology, that is, what Paul thought he was thinking about. Clearly, therefore, the coercion of the evidence into this structural pattern derives from the work of Lévi-Strauss, rather than from the Pauline material under scrutiny. It is wholly arbitrary in its approach and in its results, and omits consideration of what sociologists would consider to be responsible social-scientific methods.

Another type of interpretation of the New Testament which forces the material into an arbitrary, imposed pattern is that of the Marxists, who analyze the biblical material and the historical background along the lines of economic determinism. An example of this approach is found in Fernando Belo, who wrote:[95] "The gospel will make us hear the promise of blessing: the promise of a radically communist social formation that stakes everything on use value, or the corporality of the agents, on the textual materiality of the signifiers of the various process of writings. It is a promise, however, that is not to be awaited as a pure wager or a distant utopian horizon, but that is to be read as already realized from a practice according to the debt system, a practice that is international or catholic in scope, and undergoing constant conversion, a practice that is a pledge of a revolution that goes on indefinitely" (267). This reading of Mark will probably strike most readers as prejudiced, highly selective, and anachronistic, since it coerces the evidence to conform to a social theory derived from nineteenth-century philosophy and socioeconomic theory rather than from an effort to inquire sensitively as to what social factors were operative in the setting of the writer of the Gospel of Mark.

A third approach that is exerting considerable influence among some philosophers of religion—and may be moving into the field of New Testament history and interpretation as well—is represented in different ways in the writings of Jacques Derrida and Michel Foucault. The aim in this case is not to discern structures, but to deny the existence of any structures, literary, conceptual, or social. As has been pointed out in a perceptive critical essay on Foucault,[96] his work began with the exploration of language and discourse, in *The Archaeology of Knowledge* and *The Order of Things*. Soon, however, these lines of exploration were abandoned in favor of studies of power and discourse (139). Here Foucault became increasingly dependent on the thought of Nietzsche and the "deconstruction" of social texts, as represented by the work of Derrida. Far from his developing some encompassing mode of communication that would enable one to move discerningly back through older layers of knowledge—in the role of an epistemological archeologist—Foucault's work should be seen "as a cultural phenomenon arising out of the concerns of the Parisian intellectual milieu. Disillusionment with the possibilities of Marxist practice . . . allowed for the appeal of the 'new philosophers' who in various forms picked up some of Nietzsche's nihilism. Thus it should not be surprising that 'Freud, Marx and Nietzsche' became the accepted gurus." (176).

In the United States, a similar experience of disillusionment on the part of professors and professionals in religious studies has led to proposals for deconstruction as the task appropriate for historical and theological interpreters. Peter C. Hodgson offers well-founded insights when he criticizes Mark C. Taylor's proposal that the written word is God.[97] According to Taylor, writing is "the creative-destructive medium of everything that is and all that is not"; it is "the divine milieu." Hodgson observes, this God of a/theology is not an appropriate focus of worship or comfort, but "is for those who don't need a real God—a God who saves from sin and death and the oppressive powers—because they already

have all that life can offer; this is a god for those who have the
leisure and economic resources to engage in an endless play of
words, to spend themselves unreservedly in the carnival of life, to
engage in solipsistic play primarily to avoid boredom and attain a
certain aesthetic and erotic pleasure. . . . A god for the children of
privilege, not the children of poverty; a god for the oppressors,
not the oppressed . . . ; a god for the pleasant lawns of ivied colleges, not for the weeds and mud of basic ecclesial communities;
a god for the upwardly mobile, not for the underside of history."[98]

It is fortuitous, or providential, that concurrent with the emergence in wider intellectual circles of a social theory of knowledge
there have appeared fresh evidence about Judaism and early Christianity in the form of new documents and the radical reappraisal
of the long-familiar historical evidence about the centuries just
before and after the birth of Jesus of Nazareth. The Dead Sea Scrolls,
since their discovery by Palestinian shepherds in caves overlooking
the Dead Sea in the 1940s, have provided concrete evidence of
discontent with the Jewish religious establishment in that epoch.
The recovery of copies of their basic constitutional documents, with
commentaries on the Jewish scriptures, shows that the central concern of the community by and for whom the documents were
produced was to gain and to maintain its group-identity as the true
covenant people of Israel's God. There were also found in this
century documents from upper Egypt which furnish detailed evidence of the issues and conflicts within the nascent Christian movement in the second and subsequent centuries which gave rise to
the offshoot of Christianity known as Gnosticism. The brilliant
analyses of the origins of the rabbinic documents by Jacob Neusner
have made possible a radical revision of the origins of the Pharisaic
movement and its post-70 C.E. process of metamorphosis in rabbinic
Judaism.[99] Alan Segal's insight about the parallel and increasingly
hostile concurrent development of rabbinic Judaism and early
Christianity[100] confirms and illumines Neusner's basic perception
that community identity was the central concern of the Pharisees,
and shows that the conflict with Christians was over precisely this
issue. In chapter 4 below we shall see how some of the details of
the finds and the insights related to Judaism in the period of the
Second Temple have a direct bearing on our understanding of parts
of the New Testament.

What is required from the historians of Christian origins and
the interpreters of the early Christian writings is to strive for as

wide-ranging as possible an awareness of the implicit as well as the explicit issues between the various early Christian groups, and between them and emergent rabbinic Judaism. To attain these interpretive perspectives, the interpreter must draw upon the insights of social scientists in order to heighten awareness of the dynamics of this process and to recognize the factors that helped to shape this early Christian movement—both in its initial diversity and during its move toward structural and conceptual uniformity. We now turn to some of the questions that this approach requires us to raise of the early Christian texts. Then in the final chapter we will suggest some of the results for New Testament interpretation which this sociological method affords.

3

Interrogating the Text:
A Sociological Proposal
for Historical Interpretation

Crucial for the outcome of any human inquiry are the questions raised as the investigation is undertaken. We have tried to show that the factor of interrogation of the evidence is central in the whole range of human intellectual endeavor, including the natural and social sciences, as well as in the broad range of philosophy, religion, and the humanities. What I here propose is an array of questions that arise from significant insights derived from the social sciences, philosophy, and recent developments in the study of religion.[1]

To undertake the twin tasks of interpretation of ancient tests, including the New Testament and early Christian literature, and of historical reconstruction of the setting from which this material came, responses to the following kinds of questions are essential.

The Questions

1. Boundary Questions:

By what authority are the boundaries drawn which define the group?

What are the threats to the maintenance of these boundaries?

Who are the insiders? The outsiders? Can an insider become an outsider?

Does the threat to the boundaries arise within the group or from without?

What bounds of time and space does the group occupy?

Which is the more important factor: group identity, or the criteria for belonging?

2. Authority Questions:

What are the roles of power within the group and the means of attaining them?

What are the structures of power within the group, including rank?

How do the titles of leadership function in terms of authority and status?

How is the leader chosen? Who is in charge?

Can authority be transmitted to successive generations? If so, by what means?

3. Status and Role Questions:

Are age groups or sex roles defined?

Are there identifiable classes or ranks within groups?

What are the attitudes expressed regarding wealth, buildings, clothing, or ritual equipment?

If there is conflict within the group, what are the issues?

Who has special privilege, and on what basis?

Who performs rituals?

4. Ritual Questions:

What are the key formative experiences of the group, including initiation, celebration, stages of transition?

Who performs these rites, and what are the purposes of them?

How are the rites transmitted to the successors?

Is there evidence of changing attitudes toward the ritual in successive generations? In what direction is the change?

To what extent and why has the group altered the ritual?

What language is used in the ritual?

5. Literary Questions with Social Implications:

What genre does the group employ for communication within the group? With those outside the group, if any? What does the choice of genre imply?

Does the author's choice of a specific genre influence the message he/she wants to communicate? In what way?

What are the themes in the test of the communication? What is its argumentative strategy? Who is supported? Who is combatted?

Has the genre been modified to serve the specific aims of the group? In what way and for what ends?

Is there a canon operative within the community? How is it defined?

How does the literary organization of the communication serve to promote conceptual and social order for the community?

6. Questions about Group Functions:

What are the dynamics of the community? What are its goals? What helps or hinders the achievement of the group's aims?

What are the tensions within the group? What are the tensions with the surrounding culture? Who are the chief enemies?

Does the group use body language? If so, in what way? What does it imply?

Is there a problem of cognitive dissonance within the texts produced by the group, or between its texts and its experience? How are these problems handled?

What are the ritual means of establishing and reinforcing the group identity?

7. Questions concerning the Symbolic Universe and the Social Construction of Reality:

What are the shared values, aspirations, anxieties, and ethical norms of the group?

What is disclosed about the symbolic universe of the group by its shared understandings of supernatural beings (good and evil), of miracles and portents, of magic and healing techniques?

How does the group understand history and its own place within history?

What is its view of time?

How does it perceive God in his essential being, and in the divine actions, both within the cosmic structure and among human beings?

Are there dualistic elements in the group's perception of reality? Do these good/evil factors assume political, moral, social, or cultural forms?

What are the dominant symbols for the group and its place in the universe? In what distinctive ways does this group employ symbols that it shares with other groups?

What are the distinctive symbolic features of the group under scrutiny?

What are the marginal factors in the community's life which are important for the maintenance of identity?

In Search of Answers

These questions are in many instances not directly raised by, or even explicitly addressed by the documents produced by the various groups within Judaism and early Christianity. Yet they must be raised, and answers must be sought at the level of the implicit assumptions evident within the appropriate materials produced by the groups if the interpreter is to perform the interpretive task responsibly. This strategy runs directly counter to the commonly employed method of classifying material, or of arbitrarily assigning meaning on the basis of verbal similarities with other literature. There will be times when there is simply not enough evidence to provide even provisional answers to some of these questions. But to raise these questions sensitizes the investigator to look at many more aspects of the evidence, rather than merely settling for sorting out the evidence into familiar scholarly pigeonholes.

As we have seen, the wider fields of human inquiry have undergone and continue to undergo major paradigm shifts. It is necessary for scholars working in the field of Christian origins to explore and test the newer methodological possibilities that are emerging. Our aim is not to be fashionable or *avant garde*, but to be intellectually responsible.

These sociological questions do not exhaust the field of inquiry for the New Testament interpreter, essential though they are as a point of entry and as a process of investigation. Rather, they arouse a sensitivity to the unspoken, but powerfully operative factors in terms of which the explicitly theological issues function. These issues include the nature of the human situation, the problem of evil, the divine purpose for humanity and for the cosmic order, and the identity and function of the agent of God through whom that purpose will be or is in the process of being achieved. The questions are also directly related to the issues of community identity, the ground of participation in the elect community, the specifics of moral responsibility, both personal and social. None of these issues is ever decided in a fixed, unchanging form, since the human circumstances in which the response to the divine Word comes are always affected by the shifting cultural and social forces.

It would be possible, therefore, to settle for a purely relativistic understanding of the covenant community and its perception of its relationship to God. But in the experience of ancient Israel, as well as in that of the early Christians, there are certain central features that persist despite social and cultural change, and despite the range of social and cultural circumstances in which men and women are presented in the Bible as responding to the divine Word addressed to them. These features include:

The antecedent divine purpose for the creation and for human beings.

The disclosure of that purpose to and through chosen agents or messengers.

The conviction that suffering has a significant role within the divine purpose.

The perception that this purpose will be fulfilled for and through a community of the committed, rather than to isolated individuals.

The assurance that the achievement of the divine purpose will include God's calling human beings to account.

For all the early Christians, regardless of the details of the differences in perceptions among them with respect to social and moral attitudes and actions, or even with regard to their images of the role of Jesus as God's agent of reconciliation and human redemption, there was the shared conviction that in Jesus God had acted to triumph over death and the powers of evil. The task of the interpreter is to employ the insights that come through the interrogation of the text along social lines in order to discern what is implicit and explicit about the distinctive views and convictions of the different stages and groups that together comprised the New Covenant community in the period of a century after Jesus. The interpreter's conclusions should include a balance between common questions shared by a range of groups and the diversity of responses deriving from these groups. The basic epistemological shifts that have occurred in the second half of the present century offer both inescapable challenge and potentially rewarding opportunity for scholars to engage in a broadened and deepened approach to the task of interpreting New Testament texts.

4

Covenant and Social Identity:
An Approach to
New Testament Theology

In the latter half of the twentieth century numerous New Testament theologies have been produced. Two main types are: (1) those that take over from systematic theology various conceptual categories, such as Christology and doctrines of God, the Spirit, the church; and (2) those that organize the material from the New Testament by major literary groups, such as Pauline theology, Johannine theology, and the theology of the Gospels (individually or as a group). In both cases, there is a tacit or explicit appeal to one of the theological options—deriving from the author's own theological preference—which establishes the norm by which the other positions are evaluated. The former type serves to confirm through proof-texts chosen from various parts of the New Testament an antecedently accepted theological position.[1] The theologies of the latter variety often evidence a conscious or unconscious preference for a particular type of theology within the New Testament. An example of such a preference is in Rudolf Bultmann's New Testament theology,[2] in which the reader may observe the author's German Protestant-Reformation orientation through the way in which he highlights and treats in something approaching normative fashion, the theology of Paul.

In the present century, the dominant critical methods as well as the major theological themes in New Testament study have derived from the German Protestant academic scene. Both the individualistic theological conclusions and the analytical strategy of this tradition have in large measure set the agenda for, especially, North American scholarship. This is apparent in the fact that so many scholars use as self-evident the categories that were formulated in the German history-of-religions school of the nineteenth and early twentieth centuries. For example, it is simply assumed that there was a sharp differentiation in the first century C.E. between Judaism and Hellenism, and that the former is more or less accurately represented in the Mishnah and Talmud produced by rabbinic Judaism. It is acknowledged that within Judaism there were certain deviations from this supposed rabbinic norm in the centuries before and after the birth of Jesus, as represented by the so-called Apocrypha and Pseudepigrapha of the Old Testament, where both wisdom and apocalyptic traditions are evident. But the massive commentary on the New Testament from the Mishnah and Talmud compiled by Strack and Billerbeck,[3] and its pervasive influence in the *Theological Dictionary of the New Testament*, edited by Gerhard Kittel,[4] show the continuing influence of this assumption about "normative" first-century Judaism. E. P. Sanders, in his studies of the theology of Paul and of Jesus,[5] though making critical selection of the talmudic material, assumes that the basic point of view adopted in these rabbinic documents is an accurate historical reflection of standard Judaism in the first century.

Overlooked Avenues of Evidence

Left out of account in these reconstructions of the theology of the New Testament writings is the massive evidence that has been assembled by Jacob Neusner to show that the forms of Judaism which are represented in the Mishnah and Talmud took shape largely within the period from the second to the sixth century C.E.[6] Although in these collections some traditions may survive from the time before 70, they have all been placed within the framework of emergent rabbinic Judaism, which arose to enable Judaism to survive the twin catastrophes of 66–70: (1) the utter defeat of the Jewish nationalists, and (2) the destruction of the temple and its priesthood. What began as a house-based movement of Pharisaic piety, following the disillusionment of many Jews with the Maccabees and their increasingly secular successors in the first century B.C.E., was organized in the late first century C.E., with the apparent encouragement of the Roman authorities, and sought to legitimate itself by claiming roots in an oral law allegedly going back to Moses.

According to New Testament scholars who ignore the anachronism of projecting the rabbinic material back into the first half of the first century, Jesus is depicted by Paul and the writers of the Synoptic Gospels as engaged in a debate with the rabbis, operating within the theological framework provided by this supposedly pre-Christian rabbinic tradition. After the time of Jesus (the theory runs), the writers of the New Testament books tried to recast the figure of Jesus in such a way as to make him literally and conceptually appealing and comprehensible to men and women reared in the Hellenistic culture. This is the theoretical and procedural basis for the neat distinction between "Jewish" and "Hellenistic" which pervades much New Testament theology in this century.

A related means for the theological handling of features of the Jesus tradition which twentieth-century intellectuals find embarrassing is what Rudolf Bultmann calls demythologizing. This approach, like von Harnack's (see the Introduction, p. 3), is reductionist, in that it claims to find an essence of timeless theological meaning behind the culture-bound words of Jesus in the gospel tradition. Bultmann's acceptance of existentialism led him to distill from the message of Jesus the call to decision—for the will of God and against the claims of the world. The grace of God was seen to intervene in the life of one who makes such a decision, with the result that life is renewed. In short, in that moment of decision the personal equivalent of a death and resurrection occur, or entrance is gained into a new world.[7] Instead of attempting to enter with understanding into the thought-world of the New Testament writer, the theological product is extracted from the evidence in a way which recognizes no substantive influence of the culture on the theology of the writer.

A more recent variant of the procedure of adopting categories derived from the history-of-religions school of thought is one that simply identifies Jesus with another aspect of Jewish tradition from the postbiblical period: the teacher of wisdom. The model for Jesus is not the rabbi debating legal issues in a synagogue, but an itinerant philosopher-teacher, on the Cynic-Stoic model, wandering from city to city, haranguing the crowds wherever they gather to hear him. Support comes from interested listeners, and small groups of devotees rally around this wisdom figure.[8] Others have undertaken to show that the Jesus depicted in the Sermon on the Mount and by Paul in his debate with the Galatians fits this Hellenistic pattern. One recent reconstruction claims that the historical Jesus exemplifies this Hellenistic-philosopher pattern, but that those who recorded his teaching in what we know as the Gospels overlaid the figure of Jesus with inappropriate features from both the Jewish world (such as apocalyptic expectations and claims) and from the Hellenistic world (such as public performance of miracles).[9] What is to be noted is that by this approach, the evidence from the New Testament is fitted into categories which derive not from the documents themselves, but from the nineteenth-century classification system of the history-of-religions school.

What is largely overlooked in many of these approaches to New Testament theology is that the situation in Judaism at the beginning of the Common Era was far more complex than these overly neat categories suggest. The same may be said of Hellenistic life and culture in this period. Judaism, therefore, was not a discrete entity at the time of Jesus, but a cluster of different, often incompatible modes of appropriation of the Jewish traditions. On two motifs there was widespread agreement: (1) that God had acted in the past to disclose his purpose to a special people, with whom he entered into a relationship of mutual obligation, namely, the covenant; (2) that for many Jews, the revelation of that purpose and the divine expectations for this people would reach some kind of climactic fulfillment in the future, or would at least usher in an era of stability and peace. This would take place through some divinely chosen and empowered agent. For other Jews, more powerfully influenced by Hellenistic intellectual traditions, it was enough to draw upon the scriptural insights granted by God in order to synthesize this Jewish tradition with what were perceived to be some of the higher intellectual and cultural aspects of the Greco-Roman world. Here Philo of Alexandria is a prime example.

Equally as potent a factor in the shaping of New Testament theology in the present century as the reductionism and the artificial-classification system has been the treatment of Christian community as a late, regrettable development. The radical individualism of existentialist theology simply had no place for an understanding of the community as the people of God. The emergence of what has been variously styled as church-consciousness or early-catholicism was presented by the history-of-religions school as (at least implicitly) an aberration from the direct encounter of the individual with God, which is represented as the essence of the message of Jesus and Paul.

Although E. P. Sanders notes the importance for Jews in the first century of the related issues of qualifications for participation in the covenant people and for maintenance of status, his reconstruction leaves largely out of account the diversity of options for Jews in that period. These may be briefly sketched. For the priests and the temple-oriented Jews, the ground of covenant relationship was represented by the temple and was operative through faithful participation in the prescribed ritual there, where God was believed to dwell in their midst. For the nationalists, who seem to have been an insignificant minority during the lifetimes of Jesus and Paul, but for whom support surged in the period from 66–70, the essence of

Jewish identity lay in the regaining of an autonomous Jewish state. Even such distinctive and central laws as Sabbath observance should be set aside in order to attain this goal. From yet another perspective, the Dead Sea community believed they could maintain the purity of their relationship to God only by physical withdrawal to the Judean desert, where they studied their scriptures in order to perceive the special relevance thereof for their group, and awaited the acts of divine deliverance that would place them in control of a renewed temple in Jerusalem. Strict interpretation of and supplements to the law of Moses controlled participation in this community, to whom God had revealed his special purpose through their founding Teacher.

We have noted that the Pharisees established and maintained their mode of community identity in house-based gatherings for worship and the study of Scripture. The latter led them to appropriate to their group the purity laws imposed on the priests in Mosaic law. This resulted in a heightened sense of special identity and of relationship with God wherever they lived and whether or not the temple was standing. As we shall see, it is precisely the issues of the boundaries of God's people which are at the heart of Jesus' controversy with the Pharisees.

The persistence of the expectation of divine liberation for the faithful, as exemplified in Daniel, is apparent in the centuries before and after the birth of Jesus in such apocalyptic writings as the Enoch literature (much of which has been found in the Dead Sea Scrolls), the Psalms of Solomon, the War Scroll from Qumran, and 1 Baruch. What has often been overlooked in analyses of these and similar texts is that there is an implicit understanding of those addressed in the documents as the people of God. The important questions, as we have noted, are the ground of participation, the destiny of the group, and the divine agent or agents through whom God's purpose will be accomplished.

Essential Features of Theological Analysis and Construction

For a theological understanding of the New Testament, what is required, therefore, is to analyze a document in its own distinctive context—and to do so not only by employing modern intellectual insights deriving from the social sciences, but by scrutinizing the documents themselves on their own terms. This undertaking must include the following factors:

1. implicit or explicit definition of the community as God's people;
2. description of the divine and human agents through whom God's purpose for the covenant people is to be achieved;
3. discovery of attitudes toward the cultural and political milieu, and whether these structures are to be affirmed, destroyed, or transformed;
4. identification of the divinely intended means for achieving these goals;
5. discernment of the nature of leadership and organization of the community;
6. definition of the modes of communication appropriate for the community.

Required of the interpreter in this analytical approach is sensitivity to changed meanings of words or concepts shared with other groups, to similarities and contracts with other groups in the Jewish and Hellenistic cultures, and to the specifics of the perception of the place of the community in the divine purpose. Above all, one must endeavor to read behind the words of the text in order to seek out the underlying and unspoken assumptions of the writer. Relevant is Alfred Schutz's observation that the most revealing statement anyone makes is when he or she says, "And so forth." The speaker simply assumes that there is a network of shared convictions and perceptions which are operative within the community of hearers addressed.[10] Not only what is said explicitly, but what is implied in the "and so forth" utterances, must be taken into account by the faithful interpreter of any document, including the writings of the New Testament. A vivid reminder of the diversity of spoken and unspoken perceptions and assumptions represented in Judaism and early Christianity in the centuries before and after the birth of Jesus is offered by the title of a collection of essays edited by Jacob Neusner, *Judaisms and Their Messiahs*.[11]

An Important Precedent in Old Testament Theology

A model approach to biblical theology that takes seriously the centrality of the covenant and the changing understanding of that relationship within the biblical tradition is that of Paul D. Hanson in *The People Called*.[12] After describing the origins of the Yahwistic notion of the covenant community in Genesis 12–39 and Exodus 1–15, where the initiative in establishing the relationship is Yahweh's and worship is the grateful response of the people, who continue to be sustained by God's grace, Hanson traces the new formulation in Deuteronomy: "With beauty and power, it pictured a people whose holiness derived solely from its center in worship of the one true God. From this center there emanated outward into the community a powerful example of the acts of righteous compassion, interpreted by Torah and inviting embodiment in the life of the people. The obedient response of the people in turn facilitated the flow of Yahweh's *shalom* into all nature, restoring a covenant of universal blessing" (176).

The emergence of the wisdom traditions in Israel and the necessity of reformation of the people following the return from exile placed the major focus on Torah, and the need to have an ongoing process of interpreting it for relevance to the current situation. Hanson writes, "The Torah in Ezra's hand is here [Ezra 7:25-26] defined as the constitutional document of the Jewish community. By acceptance or rejection of Torah, individuals define themselves as either inside or outside that community" (291). The emergence of the priestly group as the political and religious leaders of the people, with the firm support of the Persian rulers, evoked a protest from the visionaries (as Hanson calls the prophets and apocalyptists) who looked forward to God's intervention in history to vindicate the oppressed and to defeat the powers of evil. The conflict with the priestly group and its definition of covenantal obligations in terms of cultic performance was not resolved by the successful Maccabean revolt against hellenizing Seleucid rulers, but was complicated by the Hasmonean family's laying claim to both the royal and the high priestly functions, in defiance of the principles set down in the biblical tradition and in their adoption of an increasingly secular style of authority. Hanson then proceeds to describe the various reactions to this crisis by those who focus on Torah as "the central guidepost for the Jewish community" (338), by the Qumran community, those who withdraw from the mainstream of Jewish life to live in purity and expectation of God's intervention, and by the Pharisees, who transferred the purity laws linked with temple and priesthood to the voluntary gatherings of the pious in homes and meeting halls, where they sought to exemplify holiness as set forth in Torah. "Home and hearth were to be the temple, the dining table the altar, the householder the priest, and the act of lovingkindness the atoning sacrifice" (378).

Hanson's work stands in sharp contrast with most approaches to biblical theology, which concentrate on themes and epochs analyzed in terms of theological concepts. Hanson properly centers on the covenant, with reference to both continuing features and changing perceptions in the changing circumstances of the Jewish people. A return to his assessment of the ways in which Jesus and the New Testament writers address these issues of covenantal identity will be in order, but first it is necessary to survey some of the ways in which the covenant was alternately in jeopardy and then renewed within the life of ancient Israel down into the Greco-Roman period.

The Salvation History Approach to Biblical Theology

Unlike Hanson's tracing of modes of covenant renewal, biblical theologians in recent decades have been content to focus on God's action in history in behalf of his people, that is, in the past. A favorite phrase, popularized by George Ernest Wright, was "the God who acts"[13] (note present tense), and its import was seen primarily in terms of God's actions in the past. Not surprisingly, the favorite text was Deuteronomy 26, where Israel is called to recite what God has done in behalf of his covenant people, beginning with the familiar reference to Abraham, "a wandering Aramean was my father," and moving through the events of the Exodus and the twelve tribes of Israel settling in the land of Canaan. It was in view of this approach that history of salvation (*Heilsgeschichte*) became central for understanding the Bible. Into this framework was fitted the New Testament portrayal of Jesus as the one in whose death and resurrection God had acted with continuing results, reconciling the world to himself, to borrow Paul's phrase from 2 Cor. 5:18-19.

It was largely overlooked in this theological enterprise that the biblical writers never rest content with recounting what God has done in the past, and certainly not with merely reporting what God's people have done in response to God in the past. Rather, they are always looking to the future renewal, to the fulfillment of God's purpose, to the achievement of God's intention for his people and for the whole of the creation. Essential to this hope for what we might paradoxically call the future history of salvation are two

77

factors: (1) that the biblical writers describe not only God's call to covenant relationship with his people, but also their recurrent failures to meet their covenant obligations; (2) that this succession of failures is seen as calling, not for abandonment of the covenant relationship, but for its renewal. And in each case the renewal is on a different basis from the one that preceded it. If we look back at the older forms of covenant with Jeremiah's promise of renewal in mind, we see that what happens in the Old Testament is a series of renovations of the covenant, with a promise of a future renewal as well:

> Behold, the days are coming, says [Yahweh], when I will make a new covenant with the house of Israel and the house of Judah, not like the covenant that I made with them when I took them by the hand to bring them out of the land of Egypt, my covenant which they broke.
>
> (Jer. 31:31-32)

That process continued vigorously after the time of Jeremiah and the return from the exile, as is evident in available documentation for developments within Judaism from Ezra to Bar Kochba in the second century C.E. This matter of redefining the covenant was the basic issue, in historical terms, between Jesus and his Jewish contemporaries as well as between the members of the movement that he launched and the major Jewish groups of the first and early second century. To demonstrate this, it is necessary to trace briefly major aspects of covenant renewal in the biblical and postbiblical traditions.

Covenant Participation in the Biblical and Postbiblical Periods

Both the goals of covenant participation and the criteria for participation vary significantly throughout the period of our interest. The initial covenant with Abraham and its confirmation with Jacob are personal, familial, and tribal in nature. Since the biblical evidence itself in its present form shows the results of the priestly reworking of the ancient patriarchal traditions, it is impossible to determine precisely the extent to which cultic and priestly functions were central to the covenant relationship in the earlier period. But those dimensions were surely important by the time of Moses, and have obviously been expanded and elaborated in the present form of the Torah, following its having been edited under strong priestly influence during the exile. Already in the oldest layers of Torah, Moses is represented as calling together a nation, not merely an aggregation of tribes. The common identity of the people of God is symbolized and even enacted at the portable shrine, where Yahweh dwells invisibly in their midst, and which is presided over by the hereditary priestly group. Cultic conformity is to be matched by legal obedience if covenant identity is to be maintained. The goal of the nation's corporate existence is to dwell peaceably in the land of promise, celebrating at the central, permanently established shrine under priestly leadership Yahweh's acts whereby it was liberated and led into the land.

The covenant with David is in considerable measure an acknowledgement of failure of the earlier covenant under priestly and charismatic leadership during the so-called period of the judges. Yahweh's initial reluctant agreement to provide the people a permanent human ruler, thereby conforming them to the surrounding nations, is the consequence of the other nations' failures (1 Samuel 8): they have turned to other gods in the land; they have rejected God as their true king; they had to be warned about the abuse of power. But in spite of these present and anticipated failures, God yields to the people's insistence. When David is installed as ruler over God's people (2 Sam. 7:8-16), it is as prince, rather than as king, a title that belongs to Yahweh alone. David will achieve victory over his enemies, and will enable Israel to possess its own land. God will establish the Davidic dynasty "forever" through Solomon, who will build God's house (7:13). There the priestly offices will be carried out in celebration of Israel's special relationship to Yahweh, and there shall the prayers of Israel be addressed to Yahweh in order to maintain that relationship through times of disobedience or estrangement between God and his people (1 Kings 8:27-30).

The role of the king as the nexus of the relationship between God and his people is confirmed in such presumably later material as Ps. 2:4-11, although in that psalm the added element of promise is that God will enable Israel's king to defeat the nation's enemies and extend the dominance of his people so as to make "the ends of the earth your possession." Clearly the new ingredient is that of political and territorial aggrandizement on the part of Israel—all of which is perceived by the time of the psalmist in a transformed version of the covenant promise. The achievement of these nationalistic hopes was shattered, however, by the dynastic and regional disputes that divided the nation, north and south, after the time of Solomon, and by disagreements over the proper location of the shrine of Yahweh, all of which led ultimately to the nation's being carried off in successive stages into Mesopotamian exile.

Yet the covenant was not at an end, even though the prior bases for its existence—tribal unity, national autonomy, monarchic rule, control of the land, the central sanctuary—had all been destroyed. During the exile, the prophetic tradition made explicit the expectation of covenant renewal, as the familiar words of Jeremiah attest:

> Behold, the days are coming, says [Yahweh], when I will make a new covenant with the house of Israel and the house of Judah, not like the covenant which I made with their fathers when I took them by the hand to bring them out of the land of Egypt, my covenant which they broke, though I was their husband, says [Yahweh]. But this is the covenant which I will make with the house of Israel after those days, says [Yahweh]: I will put my law within them, and I will write it upon their hearts; and I will be their God, and they shall be my people. And no longer shall each one teach his neighbor and each his brother, saying, "Know the LORD"; for they shall all know me from the least of them to the greatest, says [Yahweh]; for I will forgive their iniquity, and I will remember their sin no more.
>
> (Jer. 31:31-34)

What is anticipated is interiorization of the law, including the direct knowledge of Yahweh, which will be available to the covenant people across the boundaries of social stratification. The ritual barriers will cease to bar the estranged or the disobedient from access to Yahweh, since his free forgiveness will render that kind of obligation unnecessary. Although there is no explicit indication of the diminution or elimination of the priestly role, it is implicitly insignificant, since God's forgiveness is expected to be direct and unconditioned by the cultic requirements.

The evidence which enables us to reconstruct the historical circumstances of the return from the exile presents, however, a very different picture from what Jeremiah anticipated. With respect to the leader of the people, the cultus, and the fresh appropriation of the Torah, there are fundamental changes evident. The anointed of God is now the pagan king Cyrus, who granted permission for

Israel to return to the land she had earlier occupied (Isaiah 45). No kingly ruler among the Jews was to be tolerated by the Persians, and we hear no word of David or his dynasty. Instead, the local leadership is provided by the priestly line. And while there was a central shrine eventually reconstructed in Jerusalem, the main task of Ezra the priest was to read the Torah in the hearing of all the people. The Torah had become the central focus for Jewish identity during the exile, as Psalms 1 and 119 attest.

Similarly in the wisdom tradition of the postexilic period, the story of the covenant people from its beginning with Abraham to the time of Ben Sira highlights not the saving acts of God in behalf of Israel, but the Law as the ground of the covenant. The Law is the fulfillment of all wisdom, and is the very incarnation of preexistent wisdom (Sirach 24:32). Significantly, the Law is described as "the Book of the Covenant of the Most High God, which Moses ordained for us." Thus it is evident that in the postexilic period two different traditions developed in relation to Torah as the ground of covenant identity: one concentrated on the central shrine and the cultic obligations which were thought to preserve covenant relationship; the other focused on law as a divinely granted instrument of wisdom. The latter was much more open to non-Jewish cultural influences than was the cultic system, so that features of the surrounding cultures were readily absorbed into Jewish wisdom tradition, as is evident in the Wisdom of Solomon, with its Platonic paradigm of heavenly wisdom. So long as Persian rule continued with its permissive policy toward Jewish worship and religious practice, these dimensions were able to develop freely and side by side.

With the takeover of Palestine by the Seleucids, however, and especially with the aggressive Hellenization policies of Antiochus Epiphanes, there was an inescapable challenge to the integrity of the central shrine and its priesthood, as well as to the monotheistic understanding of the First Commandment. With the placing in the temple of the image of the king as Zeus and the universal requirement that all the subjects offer him divine honors, there was posed a direct challenge to the integrity of the covenant people in fundamental cultic and legal ways. The ensuing Maccabean revolt (168–165 B.C.E.) brought about the renewal of the prescribed cultic honoring of Yahweh in the purified sanctuary. But it also led eventually to the coopting by the priestly family of the kingly role. This was in violation of the legally separate hereditary traditions: Aaron/Levi, the priestly line; Judah/David, the royal line. Although the majority of the Jews in the second and first centuries seem to have acquiesced to this deviation from the covenant traditions, the growing secularization and exploitation of power by the Hasmonean line that the Maccabean revolutionaries had placed in power led to widespread disillusionment with this nationalist form of covenant identity, as well as with the incumbent priestly family. By the late first century, the Romans had placed on the Jewish throne a non-Jewish ruler—Antipas, who was succeeded by Herod and his heirs—so that by the end of the first century B.C.E. there were no strictly Jewish claimants to the throne of the covenant people. The aristocratic priestly families, known as the Sadducees, were encouraged by Rome to remain in control of the temple establishment, which was simultaneously the most important single economic factor in Palestine of that day and the dominant means of maintaining covenant identity, so long as the latter was conceived on the basis of proper cultic performance.

During these centuries prior to the birth of Jesus widespread disillusionment set in among Jews concerning both Jewish leadership and the dominant understandings of covenant identity. Some seem to have assimilated into Hellenistic culture, as is apparent from the numbers of Jews who inhabited centers of Hellenization such as Sepphoris, Caesarea, and the cities of the Decapolis, with their theaters, hippodromes, and baths as the appropriate setting for a Hellenistic life-style.

Those who were deeply committed to Israel's convenantal heritage, on the other hand, sought ways to recover some mode of identity. Two of the most significant options were those taken respectively by the Essenes and the Pharisees. In a way that well matches what sociologists have come to see as the standard pattern for what they call millennarian sect development,[14] the Jews who produced the Book of Daniel, as well as those who wrote the Dead Sea Scrolls, despaired of the ordinary human means of access to power, and looked instead to divine revelation and intervention for the pattern by which the powers of evil would be overcome and the rule of God established in the world. Daniel's visions of the successive pagan empires, pictured as horrible beasts, are succeeded by the human image ["one like a son of man") to whom God ultimately gives the rule. The cost of participation in the ultimate kingdom may well be martyrdom, as the opening stories of Daniel attest. The price that must be paid is refusal—under the penalty of death—to participate in pagan worship, to partake of impure food, or to break off the prescribed pattern of prayer to the God who established and maintains the covenant.

The Essenes of Qumran, as their Dead Sea literature shows, took this point of view to the extreme. Through their divinely ordained leader, the Teacher of Righteousness, God had disclosed to them his purpose and plan for covenant renewal. They denounced the priestly leadership in Jerusalem as hopelessly corrupt, and believed God had called them to secede from Jewish society in order to live the life of purity in their haven in the desert, while awaiting the divine intervention that would destroy the hosts of the children of darkness and vindicate the elect by establishing them as the true and pure agents of the cult in the renewed temple. Meanwhile, through ritual washing, sacred common meals, and divinely guided interpretation of the Scriptures, they reinforced their common existence as the true people of God, while awaiting the promised vindication.

The Pharisees, on the other hand, after a period of struggling with the Hasmoneans for the power roles, shifted their tactics to the establishment of a mode of pure community quite different in style and locale from that of the Essenes. As Jacob Neusner has shown in his detailed study of the beginnings of rabbinic Judaism,[15] the Pharisees adopted two major strategies for the recovery of covenantal identity: (1) they transferred the ritual regulations from the setting in the temple cultus to that of table fellowship, in the home or informal gathering and wholly voluntary in nature; (2) they began to meet regularly, though initially in an informal style, for prayer, reading, and interpretation of Scripture, and the mutual support experienced in common meals. Although they could not have foreseen it, their adopting of this new framework for maintenance of the covenant made it possible for Judaism in Palestine to survive what would otherwise have been a fatal catastrophe: the destruction of the temple by the Romans in 70. The subsequent consolidation of the Pharisaic movement following the unsuccessful Jewish revolt of 66–70 led to the establishment of the rabbis (who were the bearers of the Pharisaic aims and strategies) as the leaders of Judaism authorized by the Romans to carry forward the Jewish covenantal tradition. Presumably, they were apolitical, at least in the sense of declining to adopt any posture of formal opposition to Roman rule. They likely continued to exercise some political power within the provincial council—the synedrion or Sanhedrin—that Romans established to give the appearance, and to a limited degree the substance, of local autonomy. Just as they were making headway in developing their own ritual patterns for covenantal identity as an alternative to that of official priesthood in Jerusalem, there appeared in Galilee a charismatic figure who challenged their understanding of covenant in primarily ritual terms, and who was ultimately to antagonize the temple authorities, as well as to raise anxieties among the civil and religious leaders in Jerusalem concerning his own possibly nationalistic ambitions. That figure, of course, was Jesus, and from the circle of his followers there arose a new community that linked him with the renewal of the covenant.

Approaches to New Testament theology over the past three decades have, of course, begun with Jesus, but they then proceed to treat the emergence of the new community as a subsequent development not envisioned by Jesus. As we noted earlier, Bultmann saw Jesus as having radically individualized the human relationship with God. As he phrased it, Jesus dehistoricized God and man, in that he released the relation between God and man from its previous ties to history. Now God "meets each man in his own little history, his everyday life with its daily gift and demand," so that man now finds his true history in his daily encounter with his neighbor.[16] Bultmann declares that only after the time of Jesus did the community of his followers wrestle with the question of their relationship to Israel. The Hellenistic wing of the Jesus movement was divided into one segment which adopted an ascetic mode of life, and another which fitted Jesus into the Gnostic worldview. It is the merit of Paul and John that they recovered in their own ways Jesus' understanding of faith as eschatological existence. Only later did the community develop modes of understanding itself as church.[17]

Ethelbert Stauffer[18] seems to have been content with setting forth a unified statement of what he called "The Christocentric Theology of the New Testament," without serious attention to the nature of the early Christian community. Hans Conzelmann[19] similarly concentrated on the kerygma, though he does distinguish between "the primitive community" and "the Hellenistic community." He noted, however, that the primitive community did not see itself as a new religious society, but as the true Judaism and therefore under obligation to keep the regulations prescribed by Torah (30). He did see Matthew as developing this point of view of the church as the true Israel, but the implications of this understanding are not specified (145–46). As might be expected from biblical scholars in the reformed tradition, he concentrated primarily on Paul (155–286). W. G. Kümmel[20] took into account the diversity of points of view in the New Testament, focusing successively on Jesus in the Synoptics, on the primitive church before Paul, and on Paul and John, with the aim of showing the historical development of the theological concepts contained in the New Testament. His reconstruction of Jesus concerned itself almost exclusively with christological issues. In none of these works is the dynamic relationship between the role of Jesus as agent of God and the definition of God's new people explored, as it is by Paul Hanson.[21]

From the work of Jewish historians of the period of the Second Temple, there is a range of approaches on the issue of covenantal definition comparable to what appears among New Testament theologians. In the revised edition of Emil Schürer's *The History of the Jewish People in the Age of Jesus Christ (175* B.C.–A.D. *135),*[22] there is acknowledgement that, while most of the rabbinic material reaches back no farther than the end of the second century C.E., "it is, nevertheless, an invaluable source of knowledge of the period preceding it, for the origins of the traditions it codifies may be traced back to the first century A.D., and sometime even to the pre-Christian era" (69). A similar judgment is made about the Targums, which are post-200 as preserved, but are "no doubt pre-Christian in origin" (70). Not only do we have a simple assumption of the age of the traditions embodied in these late documents, but the issue is not addressed as to the changing understanding of covenantal identity from the period to which they are attributed to the time when they were written down—or produced! As a result of this anachronistic treatment of sources, the rabbinic view of the people of God is read back into the time of Jesus.

In sharp contrast to this procedure, Alan Segal, in *Rebecca's Children,*[23] traces the divergent routes by which rabbinic Judaism and primitive Christianity emerged from the common matrix of postexilic Judaism. As he shows, the differences and eventual antagonisms between these two concurrent movements were not merely matters of theological concepts, but basic disagreements as to what constituted the covenant community. In the process of his reconstruction of these developments, Segal portrays Jesus as "the Jewish revolutionary"—precisely on the issue of requirements for participation in the covenant.

It is evident, then, that the issue of covenantal definition for the various forms of Judaism in the period of the Second Temple was central for the rabbinic and the Jesus movements. This factor has been highlighted by both scholarly inquiry and discoveries of ancient documents from this period. These finds have also spurred scholarly reassessment of the Apocrypha and Pseudepigrapha, the latter being now conveniently available in a new scholarly edition,[24] with the result that there is growing attention to the range of ways in which Jews in this period defined the basis of their present and future relationship to God as his chosen people. The presence of this issue in the Gospels, therefore, cannot be regarded as a late, intrusive factor.

Jesus and the Renewal of the Covenant

In all four of the Gospels, then, Jesus is represented as engaged in redefining the covenant, both for the grounds of admission and criteria for maintenance of membership. Like the various forms of Jewish apocalypticism, Jesus' message is oriented toward the fulfillment of God's purpose and the vindication of his people in the future, rather than toward the history of the covenant people or toward the preservation of the status quo in the present. Both the coming of God's rule and the reconstitution of God's people are the essential elements of Jesus' words and works as the Gospels portray him. This set of indicators and definitions involves inevitably the challenge or even the setting aside of those criteria for covenantal identity and divine purpose that were espoused by other Jewish groups of his time. The Pharisees' attitude toward the temple is not that it is indispensable, but—at least implicitly—that it is not of primary significance as compared with their concern for the purifying of the faithful minority. Jesus, however, announces the temple's destruction without regret, and with no promise of its renewal, such as the Essenes expected to occur. The gospel tradition reports as his clear declaration that God has a new structure "not made with hands" (Mark 14:58) in which he will dwell. This new temple will come into being with Jesus' resurrection. There is, then, in this New Covenant plan, no place for the priesthood, or for the temple cultus as it has been known in Israelite tradition—and, of course, no role for the Sadducees. The divine confirmation of the new structure is to be given with the public disclosure of the enthroned Son of Man (Mark 14:62). That this is intended by Mark as a self-reference to Jesus' role in the New Age is indicated by the response of the high priest, which characterizes Jesus' announcement as blasphemy (Mark 14:63).

Similarly set aside by Jesus are those boundaries of covenantal participation regarded by the Pharisees as essential: obedience to the law on such matters as Sabbath observance, abstinence from impure food, and avoidance of contact with persons regarded as impure by reason of their occupation (tax collectors), their state of health, or their non-Jewish origins and way of life. Jesus flagrantly violates these legal requirements, and defends his actions and associations by simple appeal to human need as transcending the commands of Torah. His view of the requirements for participation in the covenant is in fundamental conflict with that of the Pharisees, as the Gospels make clear.

Instead, Jesus revives that strand of the prophetic tradition which tells of the availability of the grace of God to non-Israelites: Elijah and Elisha ministering to the needs of Sidonians and Syrians (Luke 4:25-27); the Q tradition about Jonah's preaching to the Ninevites (Luke 11:29-32); the promise in Isaiah and 2 Isaiah that God's good news is especially for the deprived, the ailing, and the outsider (Luke 4:18-21; the Q tradition, Luke 7:18-23). This appeal to the biblical tradition on the part of Jesus, in full recognition of its conflict with the theme of maintenance of purity, is particularly poignant in the account of Jesus' response to the questions relayed to him by the disciples of John the Baptist. Jesus expresses the hope that John will not be offended by Jesus' view of his role, especially since John's message has been one of denunciation of those who claim to be the children of Abraham but do not live by sufficiently strict legal standards. Significantly, Jesus' justification for what he does in welcoming and healing the outsiders consists of a mosaic of quotations from the prophets: the questioners are to report that the blind receive their sight, the lame walk, the lepers are cleansed, and the poor have good news preached to them (Isa. 29:18-19; 35:5-6; 61:1). By implication, Jesus sees himself as at the opposite pole from the ascetic John, in that he quotes without self-defense the characterization of himself as "a glutton and a drunkard, a friend of tax-collectors and sinners" in contrast to John the ascetic and abstainer (Luke 7:18-35).

Jesus also refuses to conform not only to the nationalistic model of the coming kingdom, but even to the aspirations of his disciples to positions of power. This is apparent in the interchange with Peter, after he has initially identified Jesus as Messiah and then protested when Jesus describes suffering and rejection by the religious authorities and death as central to his messianic role (Mark 8:27-33). Jesus' nonconformist ways are evident as well in the response to the request that he should promise the sons of Zebedee places of special privilege and power in the New Age. He warns them that their association with him will lead to their own martyrdom (Mark 10:35-40). Both the messianic role and the expectations of the messianic people are radically reconceived as the Gospels report. Although, as we have noted, the prospect of death for those who remain faithful is important in Daniel, the quality that differentiates the faithful in Daniel from the majority of Israelites is ritual purity—a criterion that is flatly contradictory to the welcome of sinners and the transcending of ritual barriers that characterize Jesus in the gospel tradition.

In keeping with what sociologists would term the "sectarian" nature of the followers of Jesus as they are depicted in the Gospels, they are represented as having been granted special insight into the divine plan. A crucial text here is Mark 4:10-11, where in the intimacy of the circle of the twelve and the central core of followers, Mark has Jesus say to them, "To you has been given the mystery of the kingdom of God, but to those outside everything is in riddles (lit., "parables") so that they may indeed see but not perceive, and may indeed hear but not understand; lest they should turn again and be forgiven." It is not only Jewish piety but well-nigh universal human values and instincts which run counter to the teaching of Jesus in the Gospels concerning the demands of his discipleship. The theme of the wise or the elect to whom God has granted special insight and knowledge of his redemptive purpose is characteristic of Jewish apocalyptic literature, as is evident from Daniel, where the elect to whom the special knowledge of the purpose of God has been conveyed are identified as "the wise." It is they who will be vindicated by God at the dawn of the New Age. Their names will be found written in "the book." They will shine with brightness of the firmament, because they will have turned "many to righteousness" (Dan. 12:1-3). The book containing these divinely disclosed secrets is to be sealed "until the time of the end" (12:4). What is of central importance for our purposes is to observe that these recipients of the divine secrets concerning the soon coming of God's rule are characterized by their holiness: it was they who refused to compromise their purity, even under penalty of death; it is they who are called "the holy ones of the Most High" (Dan. 7:18). Thus they share with the followers of Jesus access to "the mystery of the kingdom" (Mark 4:11), but the latter are utterly different from the saints in Daniel, since it is the sinners, the unclean, the poor, the powerless, the outsiders (by standards of Jewish piety) who comprise God's new people.

Paul and the New Covenant

As the traditional title of the collection of early Christian writings that we call the New Testament implies, the common factor that binds these diverse writings together is that in various ways they all attest to God's having established through Jesus the New Covenant. The earliest of these writings, the letters of Paul, portray the New Covenant people as constituted on a basis which goes back to God's covenant with Abraham, as Galatians 3 declares:

> Thus Abraham "believed God and he was reckoned to be in right relationship" [Gen. 15:6]. So you see that it is those of faith who are the children of Abraham. And the scripture, forseeing that God would place the Gentiles in right relationship by faith, preached the gospel beforehand to Abraham, saying "In you shall all the nations be blessed." So then those who are of faith are blessed with Abraham who had faith (vv. 6-9, au. trans.).

Since the norm for covenant identity which Paul had adhered to as a committed Pharisee (Phil. 3:5) was the law as interpreted by that segment of the Jews in the first century, he felt obligated to explain why the law was no longer to be regarded as binding on those who trusted in Christ as God's agent to establish his new people. His argument was based on the assumption that God's covenant with Abraham, which was grounded on faith in the divine promise, would not be annulled by the Mosaic law, which was not given until 430 years later (Gal. 3:15-18). The function of the law was that of a child trainer, to keep a naughty people in line until they could find maturity of relationship with God as sons and daughters in the new community, which is Christ (3:23-26). Of paramount importance in this New Covenant relationship is that none of the criteria which divided human beings in ancient Israel and in most human societies is any longer in effect (3:28): neither tribal identity ("neither Jew nor Greek"), nor socioeconomic status ("neither slave nor free," nor sexual differences ("neither male nor female"). The performance of the communal ritual act of baptism demonstrates and effects their unity in God's new people, which Paul refers to in easy transition as being "in Christ" and as "Abraham's offspring" (3:27, 29).

As in Mark, Paul asserts that God has chosen to give to those who by human standards would be "low and despised" the new life in Christ. In the context of that new community are given what human beings cannot attain by their own efforts: "wisdom, right relationship, sanctification and redemption" (1 Cor. 1:28-30). The main thrust of Paul's Letter to the Romans is to show that one enters the right relationship with God in the fellowship of his people through trust in his provision for human salvation, rather than through conformity to the ritual or moral commands of the law, by which the Old Covenant community sought to establish its special relationship with God. As in Galatians, ethnic origin is irrelevant to covenantal participation, since God is the God of Gentiles as well as of the Jews. No pious actions or performances in accord with the Jewish law can establish this relationship (Rom. 3:27-30). In what follows in Romans, Paul seeks to show that this principle of sharing in the covenant people is not novel, but is instead a recovery of a principle that goes back to Abraham and David (Romans 4). The New Covenant is potentially and in principle open to all human beings (Rom. 5:18). The rule or kingdom of which Paul writes is the reign of grace "through the establishment of right relationship [in the New Covenant] to eternal life through Jesus Christ our Lord" (Rom. 5:21). The new life that opens up to the community of faith is dependent, not on the old, written code of the Mosaic covenant (Rom. 7:6), but on the freedom for the people of God which is provided through "the Spirit of life in Christ Jesus" (Rom. 8:1).

The new Rule of God has already begun through Jesus, who is even now at work, putting all his enemies "under his feet" (1 Cor. 15:24-28). When this work is finally accomplished, he will "deliver the kingdom to God the Father after destroying every authority and power." When this work of triumphing over the evil powers is complete, then the divine purpose—which for Paul implies a potential universalism—will be achieved, whereby "God may be everything to everyone."

Two factors that are essential for our concerns are evident in the Pauline letters. First, Paul's worldview is powerfully influenced by Jewish apocalypticism as J. C. Beker has shown.[25] The texts we have just examined from 1 Corinthians speak of the conflict between God and the powers of evil that is soon to be successfully completed. Paul writes here and in 1 Thessalonians 4 with the clear expectation that he will be living when, in the near future, God's purpose for the creation is achieved. The renovation of the covenant is, therefore, an essential ingredient in the Pauline eschatology. Second, the reader of Romans cannot miss the point that Paul is still profoundly concerned about destiny in the divine plan of historic Israel, the people of the Old Covenant. Paul devotes three chapters (Romans 9–11) to the place of Israel in the plan of God, and of the relationship between Israel and the people of the New Covenant. The conclusion that he draws from this discussion is to take refuge in a mystery: "O the depth of the riches and wisdom and knowledge of God! How unsearchable are his judgments and how inscrutable his ways!" (Rom. 11:33). Even though the theological outcome of his discussion is not clear, it is obvious that the place of Israel in the era of the New Covenant was a continuing problem for Paul.

Continuities from the Old Covenant to the New

Although the details differ in Luke-Acts, the author of this two-volume work portrays the New Covenant people and the coming of God's rule in ways that are analogous to the outlook of Paul. The first four chapters of Luke underscore the continuities between what God was doing among his people Israel and what he is now in process of bringing to completion in Jesus. This point is made explicit in Jesus' inaugural address in the synagogue at Nazareth, when he declares, following the reading of 2 Isaiah about the anointing of the Spirit whereby he is bringing good news to the poor, sight to the blind, and so forth: "Today this scripture has been fulfilled in your hearing" (Luke 4:21). By his depicting the birth of John the Baptist and of Jesus in ways that are clearly modeled on Old Testament stories, and by narrating these stories and the psalmlike hymns of Mary, Zechariah, Simeon, and the angels, in language which directly matches the style of the Septuagint (LXX), Luke's perceptions of the links between God's work in the past and the new thing he is about to do are made vividly evident.

Luke is, however, selective in the themes from the Old Testament which he sees as carried forward into the era of the New Covenant. And he reports Jesus as declaring that there are fundamental discontinuities as well. For example, in the much-debated Luke 16:16, "The law and the prophets are until John; since then the good news of the kingdom of God is preached, and to enter it everyone is involved in conflict"; what that implies is already indicated in Luke's version of the Beelzebub controversy, where the struggle for control of the creation between God and "the prince of demons" is depicted. Jesus' exorcisms are themselves part of this struggle and portend the successful outcome. As he phrases it, borrowing a term from the Exodus account of God's deliverance of his people from bondage in Egypt, "If it is by the finger of God that I cast out demons, then has the kingdom of God come upon you" (11:14-20). So powerfully operative and effective is this work of overcoming the powers of evil in preparation for the establishment of God's new rule that Jesus, in response to the request for an eschatological sign to authenticate his ministry, declares:

> The kingdom of God is not coming with signs to be observed; nor will they say, "Lo, here it is!" or "There"! for behold, the kingdom of God is in the midst of you.
>
> (Luke 17:20b-21)

In the Nunc Dimittis (Luke 2:29-32), Simeon is reported as declaring that God's salvation has been "prepared in the presence of all peoples, a light for revelation to the Gentiles, and for the glory of [God's] people Israel." Thus from the moment of the birth of Jesus the potential participants in the new people of God are the entire human race, with specific mention of the Gentiles but without exclusion of Israel. Similarly, Luke's version of the genealogy of Jesus (3:23-38) traces his ancestry back to Adam, the progenitor of the race (rather than to Abraham, the father of the people Israel, as in Matthew's genealogy, Matt. 1:1-17). In Luke 4:24-27, as precedent for the inclusive mission to non-Israelites which Jesus is about to launch and for which Paul and the deacons of Acts were commissioned, Jesus appeals to the scriptural accounts of the ministry of Elijah to the Sidonian widow and of Elisha to the leprous Syrian: both of these beneficiaries are "outsiders" from the Israelite perspective. The special attention that Jesus gives to women—the son of the widow of Nain (7:11-17)—the familiar praise of the Good Samaritan (a term which would have sounded like a self-contradiction to pious Jews), the invitation of himself to the home of Zacchaeus the tax-collector, the mission of the seventy (symbolic of the number of nations of the world)—all these Lukan specifics prepare the reader and provide justification for the mission to the ends of the earth that is launched following Pentecost (Acts 1:8). The connections back to the covenant experience of ancient Israel are constantly evident, however, not only in the frequent claims of fulfillment of Scripture throughout Luke's Gospel and in the sermons of Acts, but even in such details as the promise to the faithful new community to whom God has "covenanted" (literal translation) that they will "eat and drink at table in my kingdom, and sit on thrones judging the twelve tribes of Israel" (Luke 22:30).

The whole of Acts is concerned with the widening circle of those who respond to the invitation to join the new people of God. Although representatives of the devout *hasidim* (meaning, presumably, those at least on the margin of Judaism) are reported to have been present in Jerusalem on the day of Pentecost (Acts 2:5), the outreach of the gospel to non-Israelites or nontraditional adherents to Jewish religion moves quite deliberately. First, there is the preaching of the gospel in the "synagogue of the Freedmen," which includes people from Cyrene, Cilicia, Alexandria, and Asia (6:8). This is followed by the evangelization of the Samaritans, who have their own versions of the Pentateuch and of the shrine where Yahweh dwells, but who for those very reasons were despised by the Israelites, as is evident from the uniform denunciation of Samaria by the prophets of Israel. Acts 8 reports the proclamation of the gospel there, the astonishing response ("the multitude with one accord gave heed," 8:6), and the approval by both the Jerusalem-based apostles and the Holy Spirit of this invitation to non-Jews to share in the new community (8:14-17). Akin to this is the story of the Ethiopian eunuch, who had been reading aloud the Jewish scriptures as he rode in his chariot without comprehending their meaning until Philip not only explained their meaning, but also persuaded the eunuch and baptized him (8:26-38).

The next step in widening the circle of the New Covenant people is depicted when, with considerable reluctance, Peter is persuaded by a thrice-repeated vision that he will not be defiling his covenant standing by going to the house of Cornelius, Roman centurion and seeker after the God of Israel (Acts 10). Peter's visions and those of Cornelius converge, so that he preaches to the household of Cornelius, with the result that the uncircumcised are converted and their acceptance in the community is confirmed by the outpouring of the Spirit and by their receiving baptism. So basic is this shift in the understanding of the potential participants in the people of God that Peter is required to recount his visions to the assembled apostles (Acts 11), who are persuaded only when they learn that the Spirit has been given to the Gentiles (11:17-18). The climax of this shift to non-Jews comes in Acts 13, where, following the conversion of "many Jews and devout converts to Judaism" (13:43), the gentile populace turns out in such large numbers to hear the Christian message as to provoke the jealousy of the Jews (13:45). The reaction of Paul and Barnabas marks a turning point in the Acts narrative:

It was necessary that the word of God should be spoken first to you. Since you thrust it from you, and judge yourselves unworthy of eternal life, behold, we turn to the Gentiles.

(Acts 13:46)

Significantly for the author of Acts, this turning to the Gentiles as potential participants in the covenant people is justified by appeal to Scripture:

I have set you to be a light for the Gentiles, that you may bring salvation to the uttermost parts of the earth.

(Isa. 49:6, au. trans.)

Yet when we look elsewhere in 2 Isaiah, it is evident that the terms for Gentiles' sharing in covenant relationship with Yahweh are perceived very differently there than in Acts. In Isa. 56:4-8, for example, participation in the covenant is opened to precisely the kinds of persons who are mentioned in Acts as being converted to the new faith: eunuchs, foreigners, and the outcasts of Israel—all "outsiders." The requirements for participation, however, include observing the Sabbath, bringing the proper sacrifices to the temple, and offering prayer and worship in the holy mountain. None of these obligations is placed on the non-Israelite members of the New Covenant people. Or to borrow the language of Isa. 56:4, there are no obligations mentioned in connection with the conversion of Gentiles who choose the things that please Yahweh and hold fast his covenant. It is true that in the formal decision of the so-called Jerusalem Council (Acts 15) there are two requirements placed on gentile Christians: abstinence from idolatry and from certain types of nonkosher food ("things strangled and blood," 15:20). Yet there is no indication in the subsequent narrative of Acts that these requirements were in fact enforced. The theme of turning from Israel to the Gentiles was stated earlier in Acts in an even more emphatic way by Stephen at the end of his speech:

You stiff-necked people, uncircumcised in heart and ears, you always resist the Holy Spirit. As your fathers did, so do you. Which of the prophets did not your fathers persecute? And they killed those who announced beforehand the coming of the Righteous One, whom you have now betrayed and murdered, you who received the law as delivered by angels and did not keep it.

(Acts 7:51-53)

94

Luke's account of the crucifixion, as is the case in all the Gospels, puts the ultimate responsibility for Jesus' death on the Romans. Yet three times Pilate finds Jesus "not guilty." And the author of Luke goes on to represent the complicity in Jesus' death on the part of the Jewish leaders as an indicator of their rejection of God's message about salvation and the coming of God's rule. That rule is not to be centered in the temple, Stephen declares, but is to be universal in its scope. Quoting once again from 2 Isaiah (66:1-2), he declares, "Heaven is my throne, and earth is my footstool" (7:49). There is in the New Covenant situation, therefore, no place for central shrine or priesthood, for king or holy land. The rule of God is universal. Again it is essential that we remind ourselves that this recasting of the hope of covenant renewal is not set out in defiance of Scripture, but is rather buttressed by selective appeal to Scripture.

Covenantal Claims and Discontinuities

Matthew's perception of the New Covenant people concentrates even more than Luke's on the continuities and discontinuities with historic Israel, and especially with what was in Matthew's day the emerging Pharisaic understanding of covenantal participation. Above all, Jesus is portrayed in Matthew as a figure of authority, with respect to the interpretation of the law and to the determination of who are worthy to be members of the new community. Wolfgang Trilling, in an insightful study of Matthew published in 1959, made the point that for this evangelist the church is the true Israel, as contrasted with the historical Israel, which has forfeited its claim to be the true people of God.[26] In 1970 M. J. Suggs developed the thesis that in Matthew Jesus is incarnate wisdom, the true Torah of Israel, set over against the Pharisaic Torah.[27] As is widely recognized, there is an intended analogy between Jesus' appearance on a mountain in Galilee, from which he gives instruction to the New Covenant people, and Moses on Mt. Sinai, giving the law to the Old Covenant people. One need not simply imagine this contrast, since the antitheses of Matthew 5 (*"You have heard* it said of old," i.e., by Moses, . . . *"but I say* to you") make the differences explicit. But Jesus is here reported as affirming the eternal validity of the law, as he understands it (5:17-18) and insists

95

that his followers be even stricter in conforming to its commands than are the scribes and Pharisees (5:19-20).

Yet more is involved in Matthew's representation of Jesus than his role as new and final interpreter of the law. In the opening lines of the Gospel (1:1) Jesus' genesis is linked with the patriarchal founder of the covenant people, Abraham, and with its prototypical king, David, who is the central figure in the structure of the genealogy (1:17). His legal father, Joseph, is identified as "son of David," and the holy family resides in the city of David, Bethlehem (2:1), which figures importantly in the prophetic anticipation of the birth of the "king of the Jews" (2:1-12). The basic importance of the conformity to the moral commands is apparent in the interchange with John the Baptist, on which occasion Jesus explains why he must be baptized: "Thus it is fitting to fulfill all righteousness" (3:14). Although both the evangelists are using tradition from Q, the eschatological promises of Luke's Sermon on the Plain— "Blessed are you that weep now, for you shall laugh" (Luke 6:21b)— have been converted by Matthew in his Sermon on the Mount into timeless declarations of spiritual values: "Blessed are those who hunger and thirst *after righteousness*" or "Blessed are the poor *in spirit*" (Matt. 5:3, 6). Matthew's sermon as a whole consists more of timeless truths, in the form of aphorisms and brief parables, than is the case with Luke's sermon, where the emphasis is on promise of present divine sustenance in light of future vindication.

In Matthew's commissioning of the disciples, there is an express order that their work be limited to Israelites, with the specific exclusion of Samaritans and Gentiles (Matt. 10:5-6). Furthermore, the Matthean version of the Parables of the Kingdom (Matthew 13) adds a new dimension to the material found in other forms in Mark and Q: for Matthew there is a strong emphasis on the mixed nature of the covenant people ("good and bad," whether the image used is one of grain or fish) and the fiery judgment that will effect the permanent valuation of what men and women have done in the context of the "kingdom." For Matthew this is a way of referring to the covenant people, or the church. Indeed, the only place where the term "church" (*ekklēsia*) is used in the gospel tradition is in Matthew, and it appears there only twice. In the first of these (16:18) we find not only an expansion of the simple confession of Peter reported in Mark 8:29 ("You are the Christ") now reading ("You are the Christ, the son of the living God," Matt. 16:16), but there is also appended the declaration, "You are Peter, and on this rock I will build my church, and the Gates of Hades shall not prevail against it." Whether Peter is the rock, or there is pun on his name (*petros/petra*), either he as the confessor or his confessions are depicted as providing the foundation for a new structure, namely, the church. The text goes on to speak of the keys of the kingdom, by the use of which certain persons are either placed under obligations or freed from them, thereby determining their status in the kingdom of heaven (16:19). The motif of the exercise of authority within the church is further developed in Matt. 18:15-20, where the procedure is outlined for settling disputes within the church—a kind of ecclesiastical judicial system. Clearly for Matthew, the church is not a spontaneous aggregation, brought together under charismatic leadership, but is already taking on institutional forms and practices. It is not in the least surprising, therefore, that the final instruction to the disciples in Jesus' post-resurrection appearance includes the grant of authority which derives from earthly and heavenly sources (28:18). Linked with this are formal confessional patterns (Father, Son, and Holy Spirit), the institution of Baptism as a rite of admission to the new community, and the injunction to carry forward a program of instruction concerning the commands that Jesus gave to the disciples (28:19-20).

Equally important for Matthew is the other side of this picture of the institution of the structured, ordered covenant people: that is, the denunciation of another movement and its leaders—Pharisaism—which was developing its own institutional forms simultaneously, and in apparent direct competition, with the church as Matthew portrays it. It is not surprising, therefore, that the most bitter denunciations of the Jewish leadership in the New Testament are to be found in Matthew. The whole of Matthew 23 is devoted to an exposé of paraded piety, posing for popular impression, hypocrisy, blindness, and misplaced values. The chapter finally culminates (23:29-36) in the charge that the scribes and Pharisees represent that strand within Judaism which has rejected God's messengers and has murdered the prophets. This is attested in the Hebrew canon, with the murder of Abel in the first book (Genesis) and of Zechariah the son of Barachiah in the last book (2 Chronicles).

This bitter Matthean diatribe is followed by a version of the synoptic apocalypse (Matthew 24-25), which begins with a foretelling of the destruction of Jerusalem and its temple and ends with a picture of judgment on those who have rejected the messengers whom Jesus has sent out in his name. It is only those who have received his messengers who will hear the invitation, "Come, O blessed of my father, inherit the kingdom prepared for you from the foundation of the world" (25:34). Thus the relationship between the Old Covenant and the New is one of antagonism, with the claim attributed to Jesus that divine judgment will fall on three types of persons who will be excluded from the kingdom: (1) those members who fail to fulfill their obligations; (2) those who reject the messengers of the gospel; and (3) those whose confidence toward God rests on their ritual performance. Yet before the divine judgment falls, it rests with those granted authority within the church to admit or exclude and to settle internal disputes.

In the Gospel of John there is also evidence of a sharp break between the Old Covenant people and the new. This becomes clear in John 9, where the parents of the man born blind do not want to become involved with the question of the authority by which he was healed, since "the Jews had already agreed that if anyone should confess Jesus as the Christ, he or she would be put out of the synagogue" (John 9:22). The fundamental cleavage between the old and the new understandings of participation in God's people is evident early in John, on the occasion of the exchange between Jesus and Nicodemus (John 3). Although he is a "ruler of the Jews" and a "teacher of Israel," Nicodemus cannot grasp the significance of Jesus' words about being "born anew" or "from above," or being "born of water and the Spirit." Yet, Jesus says, except by this new birth, one can neither see nor enter the kingdom of God. The indispensable factor for achieving the new birth is to trust the Son of Man who is to be "lifted up." John is, of course, using the word "lift up" in a dual sense: lifted up on the cross, as the serpent was lifted up on the pole (Num. 21:9), and lifted up in exaltation through the resurrection from the dead. Trust is the sole qualification for sharing in the life of the New Age; the love of God is not for some ritually or ethically defined group, but for the world, and therefore the invitation is open to the whole world (John 3:16).

Significantly, the images of the new people of God in John are not merely corporate, but also organic: flock, vine and branches, shared water, light and bread, and, above all, shared resurrection life (John 11:25) and shared love (John 13). The experience of mystical unity in the body of Christ is vividly expressed in John 17:20-23:

> I do not pray for these only, but also for those who are to believe in me through their word, that they all may be one; even as thou, Father, art in me, and I in thee, that they also may be in us, so that the world may believe that thou hast sent me. The glory which thou hast given me I have given to them, that they may

be one even as we are one, I in them and thou in me, that they may become perfectly one, so that the world may know that thou hast sent me and hast loved them even as thou hast loved me.

In the Gospel of John there is no suggestion of authority figures within the community. All the emphasis is on mutuality and unity. When one turns to the Johannine epistles, however, it is clear that "the elder" is in control, and that his decisions are binding. Thus, as in the synoptic traditions, when one moves from Mark to Matthew, the later Johannine tradition moves from the symbolic and affective to the structured and the ordered in portraying life within the New Covenant people. The goal of the Johannine group is not the realization of a future eschatological hope, but the attainment of unity in the present experience of the members.

From Movement to Institution

Similarly, as one moves in the Pauline tradition from the core of authentic letters to those presumably written by his successors, one can see the trend toward institutionalization: The Jesus movement by stages becomes the church. The model for the church is that of the household with its hierarchical structure and its assignment of responsibilities to what we would call today a "pecking order." This begins to surface in Colossians, in the so-called household lists, and is even clearer in the structural imagery of Ephesians, and is explicit in the lists of ecclesiastical offices and duties in the Pastoral Epistles. One might observe, and rightly, that the growth of the church and the increasing pressures from outside required this organization to be developed. But one might also say that both cause and result of this movement toward institutionalization was the waning of the apocalyptic expectation of imminent divine deliverance. The most vivid expression of this new understanding of the people of God is to be found in Eph. 2:11-22:

Therefore remember that one time you Gentiles in the flesh, called the uncircumcision by what is called the circumcision, which is made in the flesh by hands—remember that you were at that time separated from Christ, alienated from the commonwealth of Israel, and strangers to the covenants of promise, having no hope and without God in the world. But now in Christ Jesus you who once were far off have been brought near in the blood of Christ. For he is our peace, who has made us both one, and has broken down the dividing wall of hostility, by abolishing in his flesh the law of commandments and ordinances, that he might create in himself one new [human being] in place of the two, so making peace, and might reconcile us both to God in one body through the cross, thereby bringing the hostility to an end. And he came and preached peace to you that were far off and peace to those who were near; for through him we both have access in one Spirit to the Father. So then you are no longer strangers and sojourners, but you are fellow citizens with the saints and members of the household of God, built upon the foundation of the apostles and prophets, Christ Jesus himself being the chief cornerstone, in whom the whole structure is joined together and grows into a holy temple in the Lord, in whom also you are built into it for a dwelling place of God in the Spirit.

The mixed metaphors here disclose those political, social, cultural, religious, and ethnic differences which earlier were major problems for setting the boundaries of God's people are no longer significant in the New Covenant people that Christ has brought into being. Similarly, the mixture of organic and architectural images of the church points to stability and growth, rather than to imminent radical change, as in the apocalyptic language of the earlier New Testament material about the Jesus movement.

Cultural Adaptation of the Covenant Hope

An analogous but more specifically intellectual recasting of the idea of a New Covenant people is apparent in the Letter to the Hebrews. The worldview in which Jesus is situated by the author derives from an appropriation of Platonic philosophy, probably mediated through Hellenistic Judaism, which we now know to have had potent influence in Palestine, as well as in Syria and Egypt. After depicting Jesus in technical philosophical terms—the divine effulgence and the cosmic imprint of the divine nature (Heb. 1:3)— the author of Hebrews goes on to describe the incarnate Jesus as the "pioneer" or "prime mover" (*archēgos*) of salvation. Here he uses a term familiar from Aristotle and Plato, where it refers to the primal source of the created order: "For it was fitting that he, for whom and by whom all things exist, in bringing many offspring to glory, should make the *archēgos* (meaning "pioneer" or "prime mover" of their salvation) perfect (another technical term, *teleios*) through suffering" (2:10). To achieve this, Jesus took upon himself human nature, so "that through death he might destroy him who has the power of death" (2:14). The hopes earlier expressed through apocalyptic language are here transformed by the use of the ontology of Hellenistic philosophy.

That link is evident throughout the letter, especially in the replacement of "this age/age to come" of the apocalyptic view with the Platonic contrast between shadow and substance, between temporal and eternal, between multiple copies and the eternal archetype. That is the basis for the claim that Melchizedek is the true model for the priesthood of Jesus, since this Old Testament worthy had neither beginning nor end of days, and was therefore an eternal being (Heb. 7:3). Similarly, Jesus' priesthood continues forever. Further, the Platonic contrast between the single archetype and the many copies is invoked to prove the superiority of the once-for-all sacrifice of Jesus to the endlessly repeated sacrifices of the temple officials (7:26-28). At the conclusion of the list of the faithful of the Old Covenant in Hebrews 11, note is taken that they did not receive "what was promised," since the final perfection or archetypal completion was yet to be disclosed, as it has now been to those in the New Covenant, to paraphrase Heb. 11:39-40. The faithful are now called to "look to Jesus, the pioneer (*archēgos*) and perfecter (*teleiotēs*) of our faith" (12:2). All this is made possible through Jesus, who is the mediator of the New Covenant (12:24), and thereby the one who brings the faithful to citizenship in the heavenly Jerusalem (12:22) and to share in the "kingdom that cannot be shaken" (12:27).

Although the imagery and the intellectual framework are utterly different from that of Hebrews, in the Apocalypse John also sees a new heaven and a new earth which is coming down from God (Rev. 21:1) as well as the New Jerusalem, which is the true city of God (21:2). The new people who are worthy to dwell there are those who have persevered through persecution and martyrdom. Jesus is the agent of these achievements, who appears as the Lamb who shares a throne with God (22:1). In characteristic apocalyptic fashion, this vision is projected into the future as an assurance to God's people in a difficult present. Jesus offers his promise, "Surely I am coming soon," to which John replied, "Amen. Come Lord Jesus."

In contrast to the speculative, intellectual climate out of which Hebrews has been written, in depicting God's new rule and his new people, John speaks out of a situation of immediate threat and anxiety in the face of persecution, and does so in imagery and language that come out of Jewish apocalypticism. In spite of their differences in orientation, the Letter to the Hebrews and Revelation are concerned with the same triad of factors that we have seen to be operative in the other New Testament writers herein surveyed:

1. the hope of the establishment of God's rule in the creation;
2. the image of Jesus as the agent through whom this divine purpose will be accomplished;
3. the definition of terms for participation in the new people of God for whom and through whom the achievement of the divine purpose is to be consummated.

In conclusion we may note that just as the devout who gathered in Jerusalem at Pentecost in Acts 2 marveled that each listener heard the message in his or her own language, so we see in this spectrum of responses to the gospel a variety of images in terms of which the role of Jesus in bringing God's rule and the identity of his people are perceived. New Testament theology must seek to interpret the biblical tradition in ways that take into account these factors, both separately and in their interrelationships. This conspectus is an attempt to suggest some of the ways in which this task might be undertaken.

Epilogue: Social Perspectives and Theological Prospects

*E*ven to use the phrase "Knowing the Truth" in relation to New Testament interpretation may sound arrogant or doctrinaire. Yet the analysis here of developments in a wide range of fields of human inquiry has shown that truth claims are always implicit, if not explicit, and that the veracity of these claims rests on the shared assumptions of a community. Trust is verbalized socially and is maintained socially.

This should not be surprising, since language is a social medium, not only in its intended function of communication, but also in its origins, structure, and philological details. Dialectical and other linguistic variants are likewise evidences of social groupings, which give rise to certain distinctive features of language and which preserve them as well. In the whole range of the sciences and the humanities, there are shared languages and symbol systems through which communication necessarily takes place, and in terms of which shifts occur in shared perceptions about reality. What is perceived to be the truth in any group rests on and embodies a set of insights and perceptions assumed and affirmed in common by its members.[1]

When the historian or the analyst of an alien or ancient culture examines the truth claim made by a group, she or he must take care to try to discern not only the explicit conceptual affirmations, but also the implicit assumptions. The analytical process cannot responsibly proceed by imposing a preset cluster of categories on the evidence into which the matter under examination can then be classified. Of essential importance is the insight of Max Weber about ideal types. The identification of a type is not the act of defining a fixed category, but that of describing a typical phenomenon which serves as a testing procedure. By comparing the object under scrutiny with the ideal type, the interpreter of evidence is able to discern

103

not only general features of a phenomenon shared with aspects of another culture, but also what is distinctive about that specific phenomenon. Similarly, Mary Douglas has developed definitional strategies for social groups which take into account distinctive as well as shared features.

Therefore the analysis of a text, such as one of the New Testament writings, must not be limited to broad generalizations, but must seek to discern the specific and unique features of the writer and the group that is being addressed in the document. This means that words cannot be assumed to have fixed meanings, but must be understood in terms of the specific context in which they are used, including the larger thought-world of the group whose members are using that term. The range of options for the meaning of a word may be explored by more traditional lexical methods, but the specific connotations of a word or phrase can be determined only in light of the specific use within the specific context. The work of sociolinguistic scholars is vital to alert the interpreter to the factor of semantic domains in the tasks of translation and interpretation. These domains are of three types: unique referents (proper names); class referents (including objects, events, and abstracts); and markers (words which mark relationships among other words, such as conjunctions). With regard to class referents, sociolinguistics alerts the translator or interpreter to the range of possible meanings and the subtly distinctive connotations of a word in its cultural and social setting.[2]

By taking into account the social factors involved in the creation of a document, there are three aspects of the setting which must be analyzed. First, the sociocultural environment in which the writing was produced will contribute importantly to the shaping of the outlook of the group, either by its members adopting or sharing the perspectives of the larger context, or by reaction against the contemporary scene. Positively or negatively, the social context is an essential dimension in the analytical process. Second, as Max Weber noted early in this century, movements—and particularly religious movements—never remain static. From the moment of founding, the charismatic style and dynamic is gradually superseded by consciously or unconsciously specified procedures for leadership and standards required of the participants in the group. The interpreter of a document must be alert to the effects of this process of change within the community by and for whom it was produced. Third, the mode of communication adopted by the writer is itself highly revealing, since what is at stake is not merely literary preference, but the social function of the form. Far more than literary style must be seen in and behind the formal differences among apocalyptic writings, wisdom pronouncements, rhetorical arguments, and poetic or hymnic modes. The interpreter must inquire as to the social reason for the choice of the stylistic form which has been adopted by the writer. Sociology of literature is an important discipline for guiding this line of inquiry.

Most important is the reconstruction of the encompassing view of the world that is explicit and implicit within a document. This is what the sociologists of knowledge have called the *life-world*. It is the shared set of assumptions about what is real and what the sources of reality, the values and problems of human existence, and the origins and goals of human life are. The details of the conceptual structures reported in a document must be looked at in the larger context of the common assumptions about the world expressed and assumed by the writers.

What are the potential benefits of this approach to the interpretive task? Methodologically, the raising of these questions and the consideration of these factors combine to make the interpreter aware of the range of human factors that are operative in and behind the documents. These factors are not merely conceptual, but have to do with social structures and values, with cultural tradition and its transformation.

Theologically, the approach can add important dimensions to an understanding of Jesus as "the Word become flesh." Although there are many features of human existence which are shared across ethnic and cultural lines, each human being is always specific as a member of a particular sociocultural context. This is true of Jesus, who appears in the New Testament in the setting of Judaism at a particularly complex point in its history. But it is also true of the communities that arose in his name, since the words through which the Word was heard are likewise always specific language, and therefore culturally and socially characteristic of a particular segment of humanity. Both the divine speaking in Jesus of Nazareth and the human hearing in various contexts call for analysis of specific contexts. Alerted to these inescapable factors, the interpreter is able to recognize not only the settings in which the gospel first took root, but also the variety of ways in which the response to it continued to occur, given the process of social and cultural change that was going on in the Christian communities of the first and second centuries. All were persuaded that they had been called to participate in God's renewed covenant people, but the details of that sharing, as well as the organizational and ethical features, varied widely.

To be avoided in the use of sociological methods are at least three deceptively attractive approaches. The first is the reductionist approach, which accounts for the appeal of Christianity by identifying its dynamic primarily or even exclusively with economic or political factors. Second is the abstractionist approach, such as that of structuralism, which subsumes all the evidence under a rigid, allegedly universal pattern of binary opposition, in which every action evokes its opposite. The nuances and dynamic changes that can be seen as taking place in the New Testament writings are simply overlooked or brushed aside by this coercive method. Third is the formalist approach, which chooses a set of categories, ostensibly deriving from the social sciences, and then forces the evidence of Christian origins into this pattern, obscuring important differences by sweeping generalizations. The misuse of Mary Douglas's group-grid scheme is a case in point, since she proposed this pattern as a means of raising consciousness about religious communities, not as a system of classification.

The convictions about Jesus as God's agent for the renewal of the covenant people and about the ground of participation in that people are social factors. Throughout the New Testament and other early Christian writings, they are expressed in language and by symbols which are part of a socially shared world. That they express the truth is a socially shared conviction. It is essential, therefore, that the insights of sociological methods be employed if the interpreter of the New Testament is to be aware of and sensitive to the range of responses to the claims expressed there about knowing the truth.

Notes

Introduction

1. Adolf von Harnack, *Das Wesen des Christentums*, published in English translation in 1900 as *What Is Christianity?*, with an introduction by Rudolf Bultmann. You may want to reread quickly Bultmann's introduction. (New York: Harper & Row, 1957; Philadelphia: Fortress Press, 1986).

2. Shirley Jackson Case, *The Evolution of Early Christianity* (Chicago: University of Chicago Press, 1914; reprints, 1942, 1960).

3. Case, *Evolution*, 27-41.

4. *Jesus on Social Institutions* (New York: Macmillan Co., 1928); in Lives of Jesus Series (Philadelphia: Fortress Press, 1971).

5. Rudolf Bultmann, *Jesus and the Word* (New York: Charles Scribner's Sons, 1958).

6. Rudolf Bultmann, *History of The Synoptic Tradition* (New York: Harper & Row, 1963).

7. Martin Buber, *Two Types of Faith* (New York: Macmillan Co., 1951).

8. Other preliminary endeavors in this new strategy for theological interpretation of the New Testament may be found in H. C. Kee, "Christology and Ecclesiology: Titles of Christ and Models of Community" (*Semeia* 30: [*Christology and Exegesis: New Approaches*, ed. Robert Jewett], Atlanta: Society of Biblical Literature, 1985); and "Christology in Mark's Gospel," in *Judaisms and Their Messiahs*, ed. Jacob Neusner et al. (Cambridge: Cambridge University Press, 1987), 187-208.

1. A Social Science Approach to Knowledge for the Study of Religion

1. Thomas S. Kuhn, *The Structure of Scientific Revolutions*, 2nd ed. (Chicago: University of Chicago Press, 1970), 126-35.

2. Ibid., 139.

3. Ibid., 28-30, 46.

4. Ibid., 62, 67.

5. Ibid., 148-53.

6. Ibid., 157, 198.

7. Ibid., 206-9.

8. Ludwik Fleck, *Genesis and Development of a Scientific Fact*, ed. T. J.

Notes

Trenn and Robert K. Merton; foreword, Thomas S. Kuhn (Chicago: University of Chicago Press, 1979).

9. Ibid., xxvii.

10. Ibid., 95-106.

11. Ibid., 157.

12. Alfred Schutz, *On Phenomenology and Social Relations; Selected Writings*, ed. and intro. by Helmut Wagner (Chicago: University of Chicago Press, 1970); Alfred Schutz and Thomas Luckmann, *The Structures of the Life-World*, trans. R. M. Zaner and H. T. Englehardt, Jr. (Evanston, Ill.: Northwestern University Press, 1973).

13. Peter Berger and Thomas Luckmann, *The Social Construction of Reality: A Treatise in the Sociology of Knowledge* (Garden City, N.Y.: Doubleday & Co., 1967).

14. Peter Berger, *The Sacred Canopy: Elements of a Sociological Theory of Religion* (Garden City, N.Y.: Doubleday & Co., 1969).

15. Ibid., 3-15.

16. Ibid., 16-21.

17. Ibid., 25, 26.

18. Berger and Luckmann, *Social Construction*, 106-16, 158.

19. Barry Barnes, *T. S. Kuhn and Social Science* (New York: Columbia University Press, 1982).

20. Ibid., 104, 105.

21. Ibid., 110, 111.

22. Clifford Geertz, *The Interpretation of Cultures* (New York: Basic Books, 1973), 214.

23. Ibid., 250.

24. Ibid., 351.

25. Ibid., 355.

26. Mary Douglas, *Natural Symbols: Explorations in Cosmology* (New York: Random House, 1972), 60.

27. Mary Douglas, *Purity and Danger* (Boston and London: Routledge & Kegan Paul, 1976), 115.

28. Ibid., 29. Mary Douglas, ed., *Essays in the Sociology of Perception*, (Boston and London: Routledge and Kegan Paul, 1976), 4-5.

30. Douglas, *Purity*, 41-57.

31. Douglas, *Natural Symbols*, 195.

32. Ibid., 173.

33. Ludwig Wittgenstein, *Philosophical Investigation I*, trans. G. E. M. Anscombe (Oxford: Basil Blackwell & Mott, 1967).

34. Wittgenstein, *On Certainty*, ed. G. E. M. Anscombe and G. H. von Wright (Oxford: Blackwell, 1969), sections 61–65, 86–90, 94–95, 103–11, 286–88, 415–34, 559.

35. Anthony Kenny, *Wittgenstein* (Cambridge: Harvard University Press, 1973), 219.

36. Anthony Thiselton, *The Two Horizons* (Grand Rapids: Wm. B. Eerdmans, 1980).

37. Ibid., 378-84.

38. David Bloor, *Wittgenstein: A Social Theory of Knowledge* (New York: Columbia University Press, 1983).

39. Ibid., 25.

40. Ibid., 48. Bloor notes that in spite of the claim of scientists that theirs is the only true form of knowledge, which is based on experiment and experience, such developments as non-Euclidean geometry prove that humans have no access to transcendental truths, (101). Although A. J. Ayer (in *Wittgenstein* [New York: Random House, 1985]) is severely critical of Wittgenstein's concept of language game, since it does not lead to "truth," his own program for philosophy is hardly promising. He considers the propositions of logic and pure mathematics to be mere tautologies, that there is no such thing as natural necessity, that metaphysics is nonsense, so that there remains "no function for philosophy but the practice of analysis, preferably directed upon theories and concepts of science" (130-31).

41. Bloor, *Wittgenstein*, 71.

42. Ibid., 48, 156.

43. Ibid., 92, 181.

44. Ibid., 183.

45. Nelson Goodman, *Ways of Worldmaking* (Indianapolis: Hackett Publ. Co., 1978).

46. Ibid., 21-22.

47. Suzanne Langer, *Philosophy in a New Key: A Study in the Symbolism of Reason, Rite and Art* (Cambridge: Harvard University Press, 1976), 21-22.

48. Ibid., 27, 44-45.

49. Grace De Laguna, *Speech: Its Function and Development* (New Haven: Yale University Press, 1927), 345-46.

50. Langer, *Philosophy*, 178-80, 200.

51. From Suzanne Langer, *Philosophical Sketches* (Baltimore: Johns Hopkins University Press, 1962).

52. Geertz, *Interpretation*, 89, 118, 125.

53. Eugene A. Nida, *Toward a Science of Translation* (Leiden, Neth.: E. J. Brill, 1964), 51.

54. All this is developed at length in my *Miracle in the Early Christian World* (New Haven: Yale University Press, 1983) and in my *Medicine, Miracle, and Magic in the New Testament*, rev. ed. (New York: Cambridge University Press, 1988 [1986]).

55. Jean Piaget, *Structuralism* (New York: Harper & Row, 1970).

56. Jean Piaget, *Genetic Epistemology*, ed. and trans. Ch. Maschler (New York: Columbia University Press, 1970), 15.

57. Richard Bernstein, *Beyond Objectivism and Relativism: Science, Hermeneutics and Praxis* (London: SCM Press, 1974).

58. Ian Barbour, *Myths, Models and Paradigms: The Nature of Scientific and Religious Language* (Philadelphia: University of Pennsylvania Press, 1983).

59. Bernstein, *Beyond Objectivism*, 54-57.

Notes

60. Richard Rorty, *Philosophy and the Mirror of Nature* (Princeton: Princeton University Press, 1979).
61. Bernstein, *Beyond Objectivism*, 69.
62. Ibid., 244, n. 66, quoting from E. McMullin, "The Fertility of Theory and the Unit of Appraisal in Science," in *Essays in Memory of Imre Lakatos*, ed. R. S. Cohen et al., Boston University Studies in the Philosophy of Sciences 39 (Dordrecht, Neth.: Reidel Holland).
63. Bernstein, *Beyond Objectivism*, 156, 157.
64. Barbour, *Myths*, 171.
65. Ibid., 66-67.
66. Ibid., 103-5.
67. Ibid., 111.
68. Ibid., 115.
69. Ibid., 120-31.
70. Ibid., 139-42.
71. Curiously, he does not go so far as Kuhn in discerning the influence of the interpretive process on the data under investigation, 114.
72. Barbour, *Myths*, 142-45.
73. Ibid., 171-75.
74. "The Autonomy of Science," *The Scientific Monthly* 60 (1945): 141-50. Reprint, in *Scientific Thought and Social Reality*, ed. Fred Schwartz (New York: International Universities Press, 1974), 19-23.
75. Michael Polanyi, "On the Introduction of Science into Moral Subjects," in *Scientific Thought and Social Reality*, ed. Schwartz, 80.
76. Loren Eiseley, *The Immense Journey* (New York: Random House, 1957 [1946]), 13.

2. Sociological Approaches to New Testament Interpretation: Survey, Critique, Proposal

1. Among the most useful earlier surveys of sociological approaches to New Testament studies are: John G. Gager, *Kingdom and Community: The Social World of Early Christianity* (Englewood Cliffs, N.J.: Prentice-Hall, 1975); and Robin Scroggs, "The Sociological Interpretation of the New Testament: The Present State of Research." *New Testament Studies* 26, no. 2 (1980): 164-79.
2. M. Rostovtzeff, *The Social and Economic History of the Hellenistic World* (Oxford: Clarendon Press, 1941); *The Social and Economic History of the Roman World* (Oxford: Clarendon Press, 1926).
3. Victor Tcherikover, *Hellenistic Civilization and the Jews* (New York: Atheneum, 1974); and Michael Grant, *The Jews in the Roman World* (New York: Charles Scribner's Sons, 1973). A recent study, strongly influenced by the German history-of-religions categories, is that of Helmut Koester in his *Introduction to the New Testament*, Vol. 1, *History, Culture, and Religion of the Hellenistic Age* (Philadelphia: Fortress Press, 1982).
4. A good example of this descriptive type of study is Bo Reicke's, *The New Testament Era* (Philadelphia: Fortress Press, 1968). It includes a

characteristic bibliography of studies of Palestine in the time of Jesus and of the Roman world in the first and second centuries.

5. Comprehensive studies of Judaism that are flawed in this way include E. Schuerer, *A History of the Jewish People in the Time of Jesus Christ.* Vol. 1, rev. and ed. Geza Vermes, Fergus Millar, et al. (Edinburgh: T. & T. Clark, 1973); and *Compendia Rerum Judicarum, The Jewish People in the First Century,* ed. S. Safrai and M. Stern, 2 vols. (Assen, Neth.: Van Gorcum; Philadelphia: Fortress Press, 1974–76).

6. The prime example of this is Rudolf Bultmann's *Primitive Christianity in Its Contemporary Setting* (Cleveland: Meridian, 1973; Philadelphia: Fortress Press, 1980).

7. Robert M. Grant, *Early Christianity and Society* (New York: Harper & Row, 1977).

8. Abraham J. Malherbe, *Social Aspects of Early Christianity* (Philadelphia: Fortress Press, 1983 [1977]), 46-59.

9. Ibid., 57-59.

10. Ibid., 21.

11. Wayne A. Meeks, *The First Urban Christians: The Social World of the Apostle Paul* (New Haven: Yale University Press, 1983), 164.

12. Meeks, *The Moral World of the First Christians* (Philadelphia: Westminster Press, 1986).

13. Ramsay MacMullen, *Enemies of the Roman Order: Treason, Unrest, and Alienation in the Empire* (Cambridge: Harvard University Press, 1966).

14. MacMullen, *Roman Social Relations* (New Haven: Yale University Press, 1974).

15. MacMullen, *Christianizing the Roman Empire* (New Haven: Yale University Press, 1984).

16. E. A. Judge, *The Social Pattern of Christian Groups in the First Century: Some Prolegomena to the Study of New Testament Ideas of Social Obligation* (London: Tyndale Press, 1960).

17. Derek Tidball, *The Social Context of the New Testament* (Grand Rapids: Zondervan, 1984).

18. Emile Durkheim, *The Elementary Forms of the Religious Life* (New York: Free Press of Glencoe, 1965), 22, 59.

19. Max Weber, *The Methodology of the Social Sciences,* trans. E. R. Shils and H. A. Finch (New York: Free Press of Glencoe, 1949), 78.

20. Ibid., 93-94.

21. Max Weber, *From Max Weber,* trans. and ed. H. H. Gerth and C. W. Mills (New York: Cambridge University Press, 1977), 245, 247-48, 269.

22. Susan Hekman, *Weber, the Ideal Type, and Contemporary Social Theory* (Notre Dame: Notre Dame University Press, 1983).

23. Thomas S. Kuhn, *The Essential Tension* (Chicago: University of Chicago Press, 1978).

24. Ibid., 337.

25. Gerd Theissen, *The Sociology of Early Palestinian Christianity* (Philadelphia: Fortress Press, 1978). See also Martin Hengel, *The Charismatic Leader and His Followers* (Edinburgh: T. & T. Clark, 1981). An important study of the social setting of early Christianity is to be found in Joachim

Notes

Jeremias, *Jerusalem in the Time of Jesus: An Investigation into the Economic and Social Conditions During the New Testament Period*, 3d ed., trans. F. and C. Cave. (Philadelphia: Fortress Press, 1969). Important as these works are, they do not engage in social theory to account for the dynamic of the early Christian movement.

26. Theissen, *The Social Setting of Pauline Christianity*, trans. and introduction by John H. Schuetz. (Philadelphia: Fortress Press, 1982).

27. Jonathan H. Turner, *The Structure of Sociological Theory*, 3 vols. (Homewood, Ill.: Dorsey Press, 1982).

28. S. N. Eisenstadt, *Social Differentiation and Stratification* (Glenview, Ill.: 1971); and Gerhard E. Lenski, *Power and Privilege: A Theory of Social Stratification* (New York: McGraw-Hill, 1966).

29. Louis Kriesberg, *The Sociology of Social Conflict* (Englewood Cliffs, N.J.: Prentice-Hall, 1973).

30. Louis Coser, *Continuities in the Study of Social Conflict* (New York: Free Press of Glencoe, 1967).

31. John H. Schuetz, *Paul and the Anatomy of Apostolic Authority* (New York: Cambridge University Press, 1975). Bengt Holmberg, *Paul and Power: The Structure of Authority in the Primitive Churches as Reflected in the Pauline Epistles* (Philadelphia: Fortress Press, 1980).

32. Talcott Parsons, *The Structure of Social Action* (Glencoe, Ill.: Free Press, 1949).

33. T. F. Carney, *The Shape of the Past: Models and Antiquity* (Lawrence, Kan.: Coronado Press, 1975).

34. Roland Robertson, *The Sociological Interpretation of Religion* (New York: Basic Books, 1972).

35. Emile Durkheim, *The Elementary Forms of Religious Life* (New York: Free Press of Glencoe, 1965), 22.

36. E. E. Evans-Pritchard, *Social Anthropology and Other Essays* (New York: Free Press of Glencoe, 1962).

37. Ibid., 184.

38. Lucy Mair, *An Introduction to Social Anthropology*, 2d ed. (Oxford: Clarendon Press, 1972).

39. Geertz, *Interpretation*.

40. Ibid., 126-27.

41. Hans J. Mol, *Identity and the Sacred* (New York: Free Press of Glencoe, 1977).

42. Leon Festinger et al., *When Prophecy Fails* (New York: Harper & Brothers, 1956).

43. Norman Cohn, *The Pursuit of the Millennium*, 2d ed. (New York: Harper & Row, 1961).

44. Peter Worsley, *The Trumpet Shall Sound*, 2d ed. (New York: Schocken Books, 1968).

45. Kenelm Burridge, *New Heaven, New Earth* (New York: Schocken Books, 1969).

46. Bryan Wilson, *Magic and the Millennium* (New York: Harper & Row, 1973).

47. John Gager, *Kingdom and Community: The Social World of Early Christianity* (Englewood Cliffs, N.J.: Prentice-Hall, 1975).

48. H. C. Kee, *Community of the New Age: Studies in Mark's Gospel*, 2d ed. (Macon, Ga.: Mercer. 1983).

49. Mary Douglas, *Purity and Danger* (Boston and London: Routledge & Kegan Paul, 1976).

50. Douglas, *Natural Symbols*, 72. These briefly formulated 194 distinctions derive from her later essay in *Essays in the Sociology of Perception* (Boston and London: Routledge & Kegan Paul, 1982), 3-4.

51. Ibid., *Essays*, 1.

52. Ibid., *Essays*, 5.

53. Ibid., *Essays*, 2, 195.

54. Bruce Malina, in *The New Testament World: Insights from Cultural Anthropology* (Atlanta: John Knox Press, 1981), makes constructive use of insights from anthropology, but posits the existence of "the first century Mediterranean world" as an entity, leaving out of account the range of social and cultural worlds that were represented at that time in the Greco-Roman world and among the various Jewish groups, as well. In his later work, *Christian Origins and Cultural Anthropology* (Atlanta: John Knox Press, 1986) he largely limits his analysis of the diverse groups in early Christianity to the group/grid scheme of Mary Douglas, whether dealing with questions of law, literary modes, leadership, or group identity. He uses her scheme as a system of classification of evidence, which seems to be contrary to her explicit point that she has intended that this pattern would reduce social variations "to a few grand types," as a way of sensitizing the analyst to the sorts of factors to look for in examining a specific case. She is not offering a scheme for categorization, which is what Malina seems to be engaged in.

55. John H. Elliott, *A Home for the Homeless: A Sociological Exegesis of I Peter* (Philadelphia: Fortress Press, 1981). It is surprising that Elliott, whose independent work on 1 Peter was so fruitful in method and substance, should have shifted in his subsequent work from the sensitive reconstruction of the social content of a New Testament book to the categorization processes of Malina and Jerome Neyrey. The mechanics of these so-called "research operations" are set forth in a collection of essays edited by Elliott, with contributions from Malina and Neyrey, in *Semeia* 35, ed. J. H. Elliott, *Social Scientific Criticism of the New Testament and the Social World* (Atlanta: Scholars Press, 1986).

56. H. C. Kee, *Community of the New Age*.

57. Richard A. Horsley and John S. Hanson, *Bandits, Prophets and Messiahs: Popular Movements at the Time of Jesus* (Minneapolis: Winston Press, 1985).

58. Eric Hobsbawm, *Bandits* (New York: Pantheon Books, 1981).

59. Anthony Saldarini, *Pharisees, Scribes and Sadducees in Palestinian Society* (Wilmington, Del.: Michael Glazier, 1989).

60. Ronald F. Hock, *The Social Context of Paul's Ministry: Tentmaking and Apostleship* (Philadelphia: Fortress Press, 1980).

Notes

61. John Koenig, *New Testament Hospitality: Partnership with Strangers as Promise and Mission* (Philadelphia: Fortress Press, 1985).

62. J. Paul Sampley, *Pauline Partnership in Christ* (Philadelphia: Fortress Press, 1980).

63. Schutz, *On Phenomenology and Social Relations.*

64. Schutz and Luckmann, *Structures of the Life-World.*

65. Berger, *The Sacred Canopy.*

66. Berger and Luckmann, *Social Construction,* 92-94.

67. Ibid., 100-103.

68. Ibid., 92-94.

69. Robert Wuthnow, Mary Douglas, Michel Foucault, and Juergen Habermas, *Cultural Analysis* (Boston and London: Routledge & Kegan Paul, 1984).

70. Mary Douglas, *Essays* in the *Sociology of Perception.*

71. H. C. Kee, *Christian Origins in Sociological Perspective* (Philadelphia: Westminster Press, 1980).

72. Kee, *Miracle in the Early Christian World.*

73. Kee, *Medicine, Miracle, and Magic in New Testament Times* (New York and Cambridge: Cambridge University Press, 1986).

74. William Labov, *Sociolinguistic Patterns* (Philadelphia: University of Pennsylvania Press, 1972), 3.

75. Dell Hymes, *Foundations in Linguistics: An Ethnographic Approach* (Philadelphia: University of Pennsylvania Press, 1974).

76. Lesley Milroy, *Language and Social Networks* (Oxford: Basil Blackwell & Mott, 1980), 7.

77. John J. Gumperz, *Language and Social Identity* (Cambridge: Cambridge University Press, 1982).

78. R. B. LePage and Andree Tabouret-Keller, *Acts of Social Identity* (Cambridge: Cambridge University Press, 1985).

79. Gerhard Kittel, *Theological Dictionary of the New Testament,* 10 vols. (Grand Rapids: Wm. B. Eerdmans, 1964–86).

80. Nida, *Toward a Science of Translation.* (Leiden: E. J. Brill, 1964).

81. Nida, *Exploring Semantic Structures* (Munich, 1975), 177.

82. Nida, *Sociolinguistics and Communication* (New York and Stuttgart: United Bible Societies, 1986).

83. Nida, *Greek-English Lexicon of the New Testament Based on Semantic Domains,* ed. Johannes P. Louw and Eugene A. Nida, 2 vols. (New York: United Bible Societies, 1988).

84. David Bloor, *Wittgenstein.*

85. Hans Gadamer, *Truth and Method* (New York: Continuum, 1975).

86. Susan J. Hekman, *Hermeneutics and the Sociology of Knowledge* (Notre Dame: Notre Dame University Press, 1986), 91-159.

87. Anthony Thiselton, *The Two Horizons* (Grand Rapids: Wm. B. Eerdmans, 1980).

88. Richard J. Bernstein, *Beyond Objectivism and Relativism: Science, Hermeneutics and Praxis* (Philadelphia: University of Pennsylvania Press, 1983).

89. Hekman, *Hermeneutics.*

90. Ian G. Barbour, *Myths.*

91. Nelson Goodman, *Ways of Worldmaking.*

92. Hekman, *Hermeneutics.*

93. François Bovon, *Analyse Structurale et Exegese Biblique* (Neuchatel, 1971).

94. Daniel Patte, *Paul's Faith and the Power of the Gospel: A Structuralist Introduction to the Pauline Letters* (Philadelphia: Fortress Press, 1983).

95. Fernando Belo, *A Materialist Reading of the Gospel of Mark* (Maryknoll, N.Y.: Orbis Books, 1981).

96. R. Wuthnow, *Cultural Analysis* (Boston and London: Routledge & Kegan Paul, 1984).

97. In Mark C. Taylor, *Erring: A Postmodern A/Theology* (Chicago: University of Chicago Press, 1984).

98. Review by Peter C. Hodgson, in *Religious Studies Review* 12, no. 3 (1986): 256-59.

99. Among the numerous writings of Jacob Neusner, some of which are especially relevant for the rethinking of the concurrent development of rabbinic Judaism and early Christianity are:

The Pharisees: Rabbinic Perspectives (New York: KAV, 1973).

Method and Meaning in Ancient Judaism, Brown Judaic Studies 10 (Chico, Calif.: Scholars Press, 1979).

Method and Meaning in Ancient Judaism, Brown Judaic Studies 15 (Chico, Calif.: Scholars Press, 1981).

Formative Judaism: Religious, Historical and Literary Studies, Brown Judaic Studies 37 (Chico, Calif.: Scholars Press, 1982).

Formative Judaism: Revising the Written Records of a Nascent Religion, Brown Judaic Studies 91 (Chico, Calif.: Scholars Press, 1985).

100. Alan Segal, *Rebecca's Children: Judaism and Christianity in the Roman World* (Cambridge: Harvard University Press, 1986).

3. Interrogating the Text: A Sociological Proposal for Historical Interpretation

1. The questions proposed here were developed through the sessions of a Seminar for College Teachers, funded by the National Endowment for the Humanities, which was held at Boston University during the summer of 1986, under the leadership of the author of this volume. The material was brought together by Professor John E. Stanley, but represents the outcome of the presentations and discussions by the leader and the members of the seminar.

4. Covenant and Social Identity: An Approach to New Testament Theology

1. Typical of this variety of New Testament theologies is that of Ethelbert Stauffer, *New Testament Theology*, trans. John Marsh (London: SCM Press, 1955).

Notes

2. Rudolf Bultmann, *Theology of the New Testament*, 2 vols., trans. Kendrick Grobel (New York: Charles Scribner's Sons, 1951-55).

3. Strack and Billerbeck, *Kommentar zum neuen testament aus Talmud und Midrasch*, 5 vols. (Munich: C. H. Beck'sche Verlags buch handlung, 1922-28).

4. *Theological Dictionary of the New Testament*, 10 vols., ed. Gerhard Kittel, trans. G. Bromiley (Grand Rapids: Wm. B. Eerdmans, 1964-76).

5. E. P. Sanders, *Paul and Palestinian Judaism* (Philadelphia: Fortress Press, 1977); *Jesus and Judaism* (Philadelphia: Fortress Press, 1985).

6. Of the scores of books which Jacob Neusner has written, including translations of major Jewish texts, the following are most directly relevant to the concerns of this volume: *The Rabbinic Traditions about the Pharisees before 70*, 3 vols. (Leiden, Neth.: E. J. Brill, 1971); a condensed version of this study, *The Pharisees: Rabbinic Perspectives* (New York,: KAV, 1985); *Meaning and Method in Ancient Judaism* (Chico, Calif.: Scholars Press, 1981); *Formative Judaism: Religious, Historical and Literary Studies*, Fifth Series (Chico, Calif.: Scholars Press, 1985). Also directly relevant is a collection of essays edited by Jacob Neusner, *Judaisms and their Messiahs* (New York: Cambridge University Press, 1987); see note 11 below.

7. Rudolf Bultmann, et al., *Kerygma and Myth: A Theological Debate*, trans. Reginald Fuller (New York: Harper & Row, 1961).

8. The classic statement of this reconstruction of Jesus' public ministry is that of Gerd Theissen, which was first available in English under the significant title, "Itinerant Radicals," in *Radical Religion* 2, nos. 2 and 3 (1975): 84-93.

9. Burton L. Mack, *A Myth of Christian Innocence* (Philadelphia: Fortress Press, 1988).

10. Schutz and Luckmann, *Structures of the Life-World*, 7, 241.

11. Jacob Neusner, *Judaisms and Their Messiahs at the Turn of the Christian Era*, ed. Jacob Neusner, William Scott Green, and Ernest S. Frerichs (Cambridge and New York: Cambridge University Press, 1987).

12. Paul David Hanson, *The People Called: The Growth of Community in the Bible* (San Francisco: Harper & Row, 1986).

13. George Ernest Wright, *The God Who Acts: Biblical Theology as Recital* (London: SCM Press, 1952).

14. For discussion of apocalyptic as a social movement see John Gager, *Kingdom and Community* (Prentice-Hall, 1975); K. O. L. Burridge, *New Heaven New Earth: A Study of Millennarian Activities* (Basil Blackwell, 1980); and my discussion of the subject, together with additional bibliography in my *Christian Origins in Sociological Perspective*.

15. Jacob Neusner, *The Rabbinic Traditions about the Pharisees before 70*, 3 vols. (Leiden, Neth.: E. J. Brill, 1971). A selection of this work can be found in Jacob Neusner, *The Pharisees: Rabbinic Perspectives* (New York: KTAV, 1985).

16. Rudolf Bultmann, *Theology of the New Testament*, 1:25-26.

17. Ibid., 2:11-118.

18. Ethelbert Stauffer, *New Testament Theology* (New York: Macmillan Co., 1955).

19. Hans Conzelmann, *An Outline of the Theology of the New Testament* (London: SCM Press, 1969).

20. W. G. Kummel, *Theology of the New Testament* (Nashville: Abingdon Press, 1973).

21. P. D. Hanson, *The People Called* (San Francisco: Harper & Row, 1986).

22. Emil Schürer, *The History of the Jewish People in the Age of Jesus Christ (175 B.C.–A.D. 135),* rev. and ed. Geza Vermes, Fergus Millar, et al. (Edinburgh: T. & T. Clark, 1973).

23. Alan Segal, *Rebecca's Children.*

24. *The Old Testament Pseudepigrapha,* 2 vols., ed. James H. Charlesworth (Garden City, N.Y.: Doubleday, 1983-85).

25. J. C. Beker, *Paul's Apocalyptic Gospel: The Coming Triumph of God* (Philadelphia: Fortress Press, 1982).

26. Wolfgang Trilling, *Das Wahre Israel* (Munich, 1964).

27. M. J. Suggs, *Wisdom, Christology and Law in Matthew* (Cambridge: Harvard University Press, 1970).

Epilogue: Social Perspectives and Theological Prospects

1. This point of view matches that of Paul D. Hanson in the Introduction to his *The People Called: The Growth of Community in the Bible,* 3-5.

2. The principles involved in this method and the linguistic results for New Testament interpretation are set out in *Greek-English Lexicon of the New Testament Based on Semantic Domains* (New York: United Bible Societies, 1988), 1: vi-xx.

Indexes

Scripture Index

Author Index

Indexes